Conten

CW00594592

Harrison Primary School, Fareham

Edward Davies (10)	14
Jordan Laurens (9)	15
Lily May Micklethwaite (9)	15
Grace Steel (10)	16
Hannah Goddard (10)	17
Jack Cane (10)	17
Oliver Edwards (9)	18
Mesha Solanki (10)	18
Paige Kerr (10)	19
Hamish Symons (10)	19
Tyler Adams (10)	20
Samuel Johnson (10)	20
Daniel Freeman (10)	21
Joseph Collier (9)	21
Daniel Davis Alberts (10)	22
Rosie Hayto (10)	22
Alexander Barton (10)	23
Harry Kendal (10)	23
Christopher Randall (10)	24
Georgia Flower (10)	24
Douglas Tandy (10)	25
Jessica Lee Bunker (9)	26
Elena Gmitrowicz (9)	26
Elizabeth Lindsey (10)	27
Connor Jacques-Stevens (10)	27
Phoebe Rose-Newton (10)	28
Chloe Stoddart (10)	28
Joe Dalby (10)	29
Kira Carter (10)	29
Benedict White (10)	30
Alfred Palk (10)	31
Georgia Borrowdale (9)	32
Jake Wheaton (10)	32
Callum Watson (9)	33
Daniel McCartney (9)	34
Frank Hussey (10)	34
Rebecca Coleborn (9)	35
Luke Bayliss (10)	35
Jade Jeffries (10)	36
Adam Russell Moore (9)	37

Hannah Barton (9) — 38
Emily Shaw (10) — 38
Megan Keri Gamblin (9) — 39
Jason Hockaday (10) — 39
George Hoskins (9) — 40
Sam Seymour (10) — 40
Elena Grace Curtis (10) — 41

Larmenier & Sacred Heart School, Hammersmith

Cameron Steel (10) — 41
Liam Foley (11) — 42
Beth Dahlgren (11) — 42
Rhiannon Evie Maher (11) — 43
Lissy Langtry-Willett (11) — 44
Brendan Chancusi (10) — 44
Olivia Campbell (11) — 45
Reina Miguens-Souto (9) — 45
Matilda Cook (9) — 45
Patrick Huynh (10) — 46
Elizabeth Farrell (8) — 46
Lauren O'Driscoll (11) — 47
George Oppe (10) — 47
Banna Hannes — 47
Bruna Baltazar Prates (10) — 48
Carolanne Cannon (10) — 48
Grace Galbraith (10) — 49
Shannon Morrissey (9) — 49
Andy Williams (11) — 50
Abigail Barber (9) — 50
Lettice Gatacre (10) — 50
Olivia Hardy (9) — 51
Aeysha Robinson (9) — 51
Lucy Rhiemus (9) — 52
Samuel McHugh (8) — 52
Cormac Auty (8) — 53
Darnell Thomas (11) — 54
Lauryn Pierro (9) — 54
George Hanoun (10) — 55
Molly Spring (10) — 55
Nima Oscar Pourdad (10) — 56
Chizi Amadi (10) — 56

Littledown Special Needs School, Slough

St Hilary's School, Godalming

Jess Crathern (9)	76
Sophie Bokor-Ingram (9)	77
Kayleigh Berry (9)	78
Hannah Kearns (9)	78

St Mark's Junior School, Southampton
Aminah Aleem (10)	79
Florence Blatchford (9)	79
Gina England (10)	80
Jagjit Singh Potiwal (10)	80
Bethany Drouêt-Lewis (10)	81
Lauren Gibbens (10)	81
Cala Ricketts (10)	82
Hannah Rapley (9)	83
Ahmad Akbari (10)	84

St Paul with St Luke Primary School, Bow
Sabina Akter-Kamali (10)	84
Jamilur Rahman (10)	85
Aniqa Ferdaus (9)	85
Rochelle Jethoo (10)	86
Jabir Ahmed (10)	86
Sadia Sharmin Ahmed (10)	87
James Marling (10)	87
Mizan Uddin (10)	88
Suraiya Khatun (10)	88
Shaira Wahid (10)	89
Joel Davids (10)	89
Parnel Bemeh (10)	90

St Winifred's School, Southampton
Ajay Gill (9)	90
Hershila Parmar (9)	91
Emily Black (9)	91
Simon Solecki (7)	92
Stephen Whorwood (10)	92
Georgia Parker (10)	93
Ben Marsh (11)	93
Jessica Low (11)	94

Samuel Riley (8) 94
Louise King (9) 95
Francesca Mylod-Ford (8) 95
Frank Eardley (10) 96
Tristan Harley (10) 96
Rachel Ellison (10) 97
Euan Anderson (11) 97
Reece Bridger (11) 98
Arman Miah (10) 98
Arman Shabgard (9) 99
Jack Handy (10) 100
Adam Johnston (10) 101
Georgia Moores (10) 102
Ellie Turl (10) 103
Martinez Hart (8) 104

Shiplake CE Primary School, Henley on Thames
Sam Verran (8) 104
Paul Lyon (8) 105
Isabella Bull (7) 105
Ella Wandless (8) 106
Rosanna Pentecost (8) 106
Hattie Foster (7) 107
Leah Parry-Williamson (7) 107
Lorna Cousins (8) 108
Chloe Shorter (7) 108
Quin Wagner-Piggott (7) 109
Harry Waiton (8) 109

West Chiltington Primary School, Pulborough
David Griffiths (9) 110
Bethany Willmer (10) 111
Thomas Ranger (9) 112
Brandon La Roche (10) 112
Eliza Russell (10) 113
Josh Hutchison (10) 113
Emily Cooperwaite (10) 114
Rhianna-Marie Ovenden (9) 114
Isabel Fitzgibbon (9) 115
William Jeffries (9) 115

The Poems

My Day At School

I get up in the morning and take a shower
And go to school at a ridiculous hour!
I'm tired and I'm hungry too
And it's so cold, I'll probably get the flu!

I walk into class and what a change,
Our teacher is going absolutely insane!
She looks at me and starts her moaning,
While I'm by the door making faces and groaning.

Maths is getting boring and science is too
And out in the playground, there is nothing to do!
I wish I were in bed, dreaming of a holiday;
Instead I'm sitting on a bench, during a truly *horrid* day!

Finally, home time, the day is done.
At last, some time for a bit of fun.
Although, I do have some doubts about my mother,
For her homework is a game like no other!

Mum is a strict and learned creature,
OK, you've guessed it . . . *she's the teacher!*

Isabel Ferris (10)
Carrdus School, Banbury

The Fire

Scarlet, orange, yellow and red,
Like an angry octopus from his deep seabed.
Pixies dancing in a fiery light,
Fire, burning bright.

Dogs and cats warming up,
Like staring right up into the sun.
Rubies flying up and down,
Logs of beige and golden brown.

Lights switching on and off,
As the snakes go into a smoky loft.
Burning bright and on the go,
As the fire will burn and glow.

Hot as the sun and red as blood,
Like a red devil wearing a hood.
The whispering smoke melting my brain,
Then rising and going down again.

Charcoal as black as black can be,
Pulling me in till I can see:
Little people having fun,
In a house that looks like it's been made out of sun.

Fairies riding red unicorns,
Rhinoceros with golden horns.
Crackling noises like crunchy toast,
People standing at a fiery post.

Katie Ross (9)
Carrdus School, Banbury

The Fire

Fire, fire, shine so bright
What will you do tonight?
'I shall swirl and twirl
And do my trance and dance
In the moonlight,
I shall show my colours
To everybody there,
But not roar like a bear,
But I shall sing out my beautiful song,
For not too long,
Then I will melt away,
Until they light me the next cold day.'

Burning magically,
I wear away,
The colours I burn, never stay,
The smoke slowly dances up the chimney
For a long way,
Then, when there's nothing left,
I slowly burn away.

The last sparks swirl up the chimney
Like fairies going to Heaven
It cries for help,
It makes me sad
As I watch the fire cry
As it dies out.

Amelia Stroud (8)
Carrdus School, Banbury

The Fire

Fire, fire, burning bright,
Lights the houses deep at night,
Sometimes it's nice, warm and tame,
Then it springs up - into a flame.

Fire, fire, blue, yellow and red,
Once catching the house, people have fled,
With a witch's cackle and a mighty *roar,*
The house is burned down, down to the floor.

Fire, fire, the embers are weak,
Once connected by a log, they are not so bleak,
The sparks are like fireflies, their lights going out,
The smoke is not steam, from a kettle spout.

Fire, fire, it has no green,
It can be nice, but mostly mean,
It *is* quite useful - you can cook and toast,
But *don't* try to make a turkey roast!

Sarah McKelvey (8)
Carrdus School, Banbury

Soft Icing Fire

Fire burning, smoke whirling
Dusty icing everywhere
Charcoal swaying black as night
Pixies dancing, burning bright
Rippling crunchy noise it makes
Ruby embers glowing clear
Fire saying welcome in
Beckoning, he's the best
Wood is coloured caramel
Tingling bright, of course, at night
Transparent fire, look, it's there
Sparkling fire looks gentle
But he's ferocious if you go too close.

Holly Christina Mystkowski (9)
Carrdus School, Banbury

Fire Fun

Come with me,
Have some tea,
Be enchanted by the spinning of smoke,
The whispering of my special sparks,
Come and waltz, spin and swirl,
Let the orange glow take you by the hand,
Let us dance, let us sing, to the gentle beat of drums.

Don't worry, don't fret,
Smell the lovely smell of swirling smoke,
Look, listen to the crackle of sparks,
Now you must have fun,
With the flicker of fire,
Come on, sing, dance,
Be happy.

Molly King (9)
Carrdus School, Banbury

Silence

Silence is like a blank piece of paper
It is still and clear and deep like a well,
Silence can be huge like an iceberg
Or small like an igloo,
Silence is a lone Inuit, captive on a frozen lake,
Silence is pure bright, white light,
Silence smells of pine needles, sharp and tangy,
Silence is peace and calm
Then it has the soft stroke of a cool autumn breeze,
Silence can be lonely and sad
Like ice cubes lodged in the pit of your stomach,
Silence is neither good nor bad,
Silence is always waiting for you to give it meaning.

Ruairi Duval Smith (10)
Christ Church Primary School, Camden

Hunger

Hunger is like lava
Hunger smells like burning fish
Hunger tastes like melting iron
Hunger sounds like a roaring volcano
Hunger looks like a ferocious bear
Hunger feels like being stung by a bee
Hunger reminds me of sadness
Hunger is as fast as a peregrine falcon
Hunger is as cunning as a fox
Hunger is as cold as the Arctic snow.

Radoslav Shopov (10)
Christ Church Primary School, Camden

Anger

Anger smells like burning rubber
Anger tastes strong and spicy
Anger sounds like someone being tortured and screaming
Anger feels like burning, sharp and spiky
Anger looks like boiling hot iron dripping from your mind
Anger reminds me of a volcano erupting inside your body
Flowing with molten lava.

Ellie Edmonds (9)
Christ Church Primary School, Camden

Anger

Anger is like lightning striking a tree
Anger smells like rotten fish decaying
It tastes like chocolate when you've just burnt your tongue
It looks like you're turning into scarlet, fiery flames
And most of all, it feels as if you're being picked up and thrown around
This is how you feel when you've been struck by anger.

Tallulah Taylor (10)
Christ Church Primary School, Camden

Hunger

Beware the beast that prowls within
Searching for its prey
It kicks, bites, scratches, shouts
But never walks away
This is how hunger feels.

Beware the beast whose eyes
Are hypnotised by the thought of grub
He keeps looking at anything that moves
Even the smallest seed
This is how hunger looks.

Beware the beast who smells the feast
But never gets to eat
He looks around but there's nothing to discover
Realising it is all in his memory from the distant past
This is how hunger smells.

Beware the beast who howls himself to sleep
Dreaming of his favourite foods
He wakes up to find it's all a dream
And his wail turns into a whimper
This is how hunger sounds.

Beware the beast that roams the ashes
And eats but never swallows
His belly's never satisfied
And his appetite never dies
This is how hunger tastes.

Beware the beast who travels alone
Who wanders through memories of food
Who is this beast?
You may ask the name
It is Hunger.

Adrienne Solon (9)
Christ Church Primary School, Camden

Anger

Anger is like an earthquake
It looks like a red-hot ball of fire whirling in the sky
Anger tastes like chillies
And smells like burning toast
Anger feels like sugar paper
And reminds me of the colour red.

Şifa Scott (9)
Christ Church Primary School, Camden

Darkness

Darkness is black like a crow
It smells like nothing
It tastes like metal
It looks like a long shadow
It feels cold and hard
It reminds me of an empty black space.

Jacob Locke-Gotel (10)
Christ Church Primary School, Camden

Laughter

Laughter is like an explosion of sunshine
And is the colours of the rainbow
It reminds me of the sea splashing against my ankles
And it smells like hot melted chocolate
It tastes like fresh apples from an orchard
And it sounds like nightingales singing in the trees
It looks like a deep red rose
And it feels as soft as fox fur.

Alicia Poultney (9)
Christ Church Primary School, Camden

Fun!

Inside you is a little spirit,
Who pops out now and then.
Its body looks like a rainbow
And its head looks like a hen's.

Inside you is a little spirit,
Who smiles from ear to ear.
It smells like fresh roses
And tastes like ginger beer.

Inside you is a little spirit,
The spirit is called fun.
It feels like the finest silk
And everyone has one!

Megan Rose Van Pelt (9)
Christ Church Primary School, Camden

Fun!

Fun!
Is like sugary sherbet, exploding in your mouth,
Fun!
Is shocking pink, dazzling in your eyes,
Fun!
Is like a field of roses, tickling your nose,
Fun!
Is a circus act, cartwheeling through the sky,
Fun!
Is like a wardrobe of furry coats, sliding your way through,
Fun!
It's all my friends playing with me!
Fun!

Eva Barnett (10)
Christ Church Primary School, Camden

Anger

Anger is the colour of a deep blood-red
Anger sounds like a million plates being smashed to the ground
Anger tastes like a flaming hot spicy Scotch Bonnet pepper
Anger smells like burning smoke
Anger feels like a sharp razor blade
Anger looks like a raging shark on a rampage.

Johnny O'Flynn (10)
Christ Church Primary School, Camden

Anger

Creeping up on me like a lion stalking its prey
Rising within me like night killing day

Sometimes I can't control it
It takes me by the throat
Darkness covers me like a thick black coat

Blacker than an Irish stout
Something inside trying to get out
Welling up within me
Telling me to shout!

It's crept up on me!
It's out!
Who is that inside me, throwing me about?

Luca Whitney (10)
Christ Church Primary School, Camden

Hunger

Hunger is the colour of dark blue
Hunger smells like steaming hot stew
Hunger tastes like chicken liver
Hunger looks like a really wide river
Hunger feels like a burning pain
Which reminds me of when the hamster bit me.

Peter Nicholas (10)
Christ Church Primary School, Camden

Happiness

Happiness is yellow like the hot summer sun
It sounds like a happy child in a wonderful playground
It tastes like the birthday cake I had last September
It smells as sweet as sweet can be
It feels like the hug from my caring mum
Happiness reminds me of my last holiday
To the hottest beach you can think of.

Priyanka Jerath (8)
Dair House School, Slough

Scared

Being scared is black like a dark forest
It feels like you're stuck in a cage with a lion
It tastes like you have just eaten a scary, black beetle
It has a terrifying, horrible smell
And it reminds me of kidnapped children
Missing their parents and lost forever
Nothing can get them back home now.

Amy Pearce (8)
Dair House School, Slough

Sadness

When someone died, I felt the colour grey run down my spine
I tastes the spices that I don't like
When I'm sad, I see a big black rain cloud
Sadness feels like warm water forced down my throat
It does not smell nice
It reminds me of when my dad's away.

Amar Sidhu (8)
Dair House School, Slough

Happiness

Happiness is as yellow as the summer sun
It feels like warm, summer air blowing through my hair
I can taste a lovely kiwi ice lolly in my mouth
I can hear friends laughing like a laughing audience
It smells like a blooming flower swaying in the breeze
It reminds me of my birthday.

Harrison Honey (7)
Dair House School, Slough

Sadness

Sadness is the colour black, like a dark night
It smells like salt and vinegar
It can taste like the sea
It sounds like thunder
Sometimes it feels like you can never stop crying
Sadness reminds me of when I see someone cry.

Macy Jo Thomas (8)
Dair House School, Slough

Sadness

Sadness is clear, like a big tear rolling down my cheek
It smells like a drop of sour vinegar
It feels like a broken heart
It tastes like a big, salty teardrop from the salty, rolling sea
It sounds like the cry from a newborn baby
Sadness reminds me of Dad going away
People being very selfish and very bad to me
It reminds me of losing my belongings
And the pain of getting hurt
I remind myself with sadness of breaking my belongings.

Andrew Walker (7)
Dair House School, Slough

Happiness

Happiness is red like a big sweet heart
It feels like a kind friend
It smells like turkey for Christmas
It tastes like a big, round chocolate
I can hear the sound of bells
Happiness reminds me of Manchester United
Winning the Premiership!

Ashwyn Randev (8)
Dair House School, Slough

Love

Love is red like a bursting rose in the summer
It sounds like bells jingling in the winter
It tastes like chocolate brownies in my mouth
I can smell mint from my mum's garden
It feels like my soft bed I got for my birthday
Love reminds me of my dog and fish, my brother and sister
My mum and my dad, my grandma and grandad and more.

Zoe Knoester (8)
Dair House School, Slough

Love

Love is pink
    Like a big, happy heart
    It feels like summer
    And it's just at the start
    It sounds like a lovely laugh
    It tastes like a fudge cake
    Love smells as if it were a tulip
    It reminds me of family and friends.

Abigail Clarke (7)
Dair House School, Slough

Happiness

Happiness is red like a huge red heart
I can hear sounds like the bells of Santa's sleigh
It tastes just like sugar on my tongue
It is like getting green, gold and silver presents
It feels like something soft and warm
It reminds me of laughter
Happiness.

Xavier Garnham (8)
Dair House School, Slough

Happiness

Happiness is red like Santa's red sleigh
It tastes like a snowflake on your tongue
It smells like big fat turkeys at Christmas
It feels like lots of rainbow presents
It sounds like Santa's reindeer are coming.

Blue Hawley (9)
Dair House School, Slough

The Crocodile

I'm a mean, green eating machine
Eyes bulging over black-green swampy foam,
My tail swings like a mace, water cascades over my armour
I eat catfish whole for fun . . . *miaow!*

Mouth wide open, my teeth gleam
I sometimes look in the river's mirror and scream!
My teeth picked clean by an old feathered friend
They shine for the rest of the day.

I think I like this life.

Edward Davies (10)
Harrison Primary School, Fareham

My Window

I was looking out of my window, it was quite dull
Then I saw a big fat gull
I knew it meant the weather was bad
Like the weather we'd just had
All the wind was kicking in
Knocking over all the bins
Then the sun started to shine
Now, out there is the place to dine
I wished, I wished that it would snow
Because the temperature was quite low
When it looked like it was quite stormy
The scene then got quite gory
It looked like it was going to rain
Then it rained, glorious pain.

Jordan Laurens (9)
Harrison Primary School, Fareham

The Ocean

The ocean waves sway about
Up and down
The tide is in
And the ocean's asleep again

As the sea creatures go down
To the bottom of the sea
The ocean sits there
Music starts, the ocean carries on its journey

The sunset breaks through onto the ocean
And life starts again
Gently the ocean seeps away
Bye-bye!

Lily May Micklethwaite (9)
Harrison Primary School, Fareham

Friendship

Friendship, friendship,
It is a great thing to know,
You need to make your friends happy,
Even give them a pretty pink bow!

Friendship, friendship,
Everyone needs some friendship,
You don't want to let it go,
Friendship is like a big filmstrip.

Friendship, friendship,
When your friends are really down,
If you take them swimming, take care!
You wouldn't want them to ever drown.

Friendship, friendship,
You never want to lose it,
You always, always need friendship,
You never ever want it to split.

Friendship, friendship,
Everybody needs someone,
Old people also need a friend,
It is as good as eating a bun.

Friendship, friendship,
I also need a friend too,
I am also very grateful,
That I have got a friend like you.

Friendship, friendship,
When you are down in the dumps,
You have got loads of friends to help
And you don't want it to bump!

Friendship, friendship,
Everybody needs a friend,
Hold their hands and never let go
And never ever, ever pretend.

Grace Steel (10)
Harrison Primary School, Fareham

Monkeys

M onkeys are our ancestors
O rang-utans, their bigger cousins
N estling together in their groups
K issing and hugging one another
E veryone laughs as they stand and watch
Y elping and clapping with delight
S uch a great day at the zoo!

Hannah Goddard (10)
Harrison Primary School, Fareham

The Dog Kennings

Loud-barker
Cat-chaser
Bone-eater
Deep-digger
Bone-hider
Fast-runner
Fast-eater
Slow-sleeper
Toothbrush-hater
Sleep-lover
Shoe-smeller
Shoe-chewer
Homework-destroyers
Smelly-pooer
Messy-eater
Chew toy-lover
Frisbee-catcher
Tennis ball-chaser
Good-swimmer
Bath-hater
Water-drinker
Biscuit-eater!

Jack Cane (10)
Harrison Primary School, Fareham

I Finished It!

I found this poem rather difficult to write,
I argued and argued, from noon till night,
Like an engine, steam appeared from my mother's ears
While I tried to find some ideas!

I thought of tankas and haikus to write as I sit,
I tried a tanka, but the syllables didn't fit,
Then a haiku, but found it too short,
So at this point, I thought, I want to do some sport!

Should I sneak off to the PS2 while my mum isn't looking?
Maybe not, she's already cooking!
The computer's looking tempting - but I've come too far,
So I think I'll finish it in the car!

So, here we are, a poem I have written all on my own,
I no longer need to moan and groan,
The steam has gone from my mother's ears
And I hope to share this with my peers!

Oliver Edwards (9)
Harrison Primary School, Fareham

My Friends

My friends are the best,
They like me day and night,
My friends are so great,
They hate me if we fight.

My friends are so great,
They annoy me every day,
My friends are the best,
We like it when we play.

My friends are irreplaceable,
Sam's the best I have,
He's there when I need him
And no one can change all that.

Mesha Solanki (10)
Harrison Primary School, Fareham

The Sleepless Night

The quiet of the beach in the middle of the night,
The lapping of the waves gave the little girl a fright.
She took her mother's hand as she walked along the shore
And thought she saw a lion that gave a mighty roar.

The shadows of the rocks were very, very scary,
But she could see the house lights and her little dog called Mary.
Mary bounded over and knocked her to the floor,
It was cold, damp and misty along the moonlit shore.

They made their way back home, it was cosy, it was warm,
She looked back out the window, there was going to be a storm.
When the rain hit the window, it came down hard and fast,
She wondered just how long the scary storm would last.

It was time to go to bed, so she climbed up all the stairs
And snuggled down tight, with her cosy little bears.

Paige Kerr (10)
Harrison Primary School, Fareham

My Sister And Her Mate

I think my sister is great
Especially her mate
Her mate is really hot
My sister thinks she's not

They have got great fashion
To me, I think it's babe passion
Do you think I should give her a rose
Or a voucher to pierce her nose?

I took her on a date
Where I sneezed on her plate
She kicked me on the knee
After dumping me

It doesn't really matter
My looks have others to flatter.

Hamish Symons (10)
Harrison Primary School, Fareham

I've An Owl

I've an owl called Hoot-Hoot
All he does is *toot-toot!*
His breakfast is usually fruit
He's always chewing on a boot.

Despite all this he's a really nice guy
I love to sit and watch him fly
He soars right up into the sky
It's hard to see him when he's so high.

He tapped upon my windowpane
Trying to shelter from the rain
I took him in and fed him grain
My mum said that I'm insane!

To you, it might be silly to say
He's my best friend - we love to play
Hoot's here for good - I wish and pray
I hope he never flies away!

Tyler Adams (10)
Harrison Primary School, Fareham

My Hamster

I had a hamster
His name was Mr Bubbles
He escaped from his cage
And he was in trouble
He jumped to the floor
And broke his paw
We took him to the vet
To have it set.

Samuel Johnson (10)
Harrison Primary School, Fareham

Boats

Boats are so cool
You can't use them in a swimming pool
I think they're great
So does my mate

Sailing isn't glum
Unlike being grounded by your mum
Being grounded is boring
But when you're sailing, you're roaring

I have a boat
It has a special coat
I go sailing for fun
And my boredom percent is none

If you have the right gear
It becomes clear
That being grounded
Should never have been founded

My family have many boats
They all have special coats
So be cool
And don't use them in a swimming pool.

Daniel Freeman (10)
Harrison Primary School, Fareham

The Dog From Peru

There was a big dog from Peru
Whose favourite thing was to chew
He went to the palace
And without any malice
Ate up all the Queen's shoes!

Joseph Collier (9)
Harrison Primary School, Fareham

Have You Seen . . . ?

Daniel: 'Have you seen The World Globetrotters?'
Joe: 'No, have you seen The Bulls?'
Daniel: 'Globetrotters can do specials!'
Joe: 'Bulls can do cool slam dunks!'

Daniel: 'Have you seen the England cricket team?'
Joe: 'No, have you seen the Aussie cricket team?'
Daniel: 'England can hit fours!'
Joe: 'The Aussies can hit sixes!'

Daniel: 'Have you see the tennis player Andrew Murray?'
Joe: 'What, that good one?'
Daniel: 'Yeah, him. Something we can agree on!'
Joe and Daniel: 'Finally, for once!'

Daniel Davis Alberts (10)
Harrison Primary School, Fareham

My Cat

My cat is called Tigger,
If he eats anymore he will get bigger and bigger,
He has long whiskers and a bushy tail,
He is a tabby, brown and a male,
Tigger sometimes brings in mice,
Which scares Mummy and me,
But he thinks they're rather nice,
He sleeps all day, stays out all night
And comes back in the early morning light,
Even though he does all this,
We love our cat Tigger
And that's how it is!

Rosie Hayto (10)
Harrison Primary School, Fareham

The Evil Wizard's Order

A menacing dragon named Gilder
Flew across the sky
Searching for a deer
That it could swallow whole

Gilder was a mean, old dragon
Killing elves and dwarves
But his biggest enemy was an elf
Called Prince Straun the Peaceful

Straun was watching the fearsome dragon
And with a bow and arrow
Stood perplexed and still
Waiting for a chance to fire

Close by a goblin, hiding
Ordered to find an elf to kill
With a poisoned dagger
Ready to strike

The goblin took his orders
From evil Wizard Horlock
A sad and lonely wizard
Without his dragon Gilder.

Alexander Barton (10)
Harrison Primary School, Fareham

My Dog Betty

I have a dog called Betty,
Really, she's very, very sweaty,
You know when she needs some food,
You know when she needs the loo,
She weighs a millions tons
And she eats up all the crumbs
And that's my dog called Betty!

Harry Kendal (10)
Harrison Primary School, Fareham

School Day - Thursday

When we are walking to school,
On a Thursday morning,
The teachers are having their tea,
Which they have just started pouring.

We are waiting outside,
For the teachers to be ready,
The doors open wide,
We file in slow and steady.

We're supposed to do literacy,
But practise our play,
Which has to be perfect,
For our parents next day.

We started games and I played tennis,
After that, we got ready for home,
I got all my things and walked with my friends,
When I arrived, I saw my dog and gave him a bone.

Christopher Randall (10)
Harrison Primary School, Fareham

Fruitful

Fruit, fruit, it's good for you
Bananas, apples, they taste good too
Strawberries, blackberries, yum, yum, yum
All very nice in my tum.

Eat five a day
That's the healthy way
To keep you fit
And that's the end of it.

Georgia Flower (10)
Harrison Primary School, Fareham

I Am A Duck!

I am a duck,
I have lots of luck,
I'm a sweet little fellow,
I'm cute and yellow,
I get off with the girls,
Because I give them pearls.

I am a duck,
I roll around in the muck,
My name is Bertie
And I get all dirty,
To get clean,
I roll around in Lake Been.

I am a duck,
I like to play with a puck,
I like to play hockey,
With my mate Rocky,
I like to score goals,
Against stinky trolls.

I am a duck,
Too small to drive a truck,
I ride a bike,
I hit a spike,
Unfortunately I fell under a truck
And now I am a squashed duck!

Douglas Tandy (10)
Harrison Primary School, Fareham

Birthdays

Birthdays are great,
Birthdays are fun,
I love it when it is my birthday,
Because I feel like number one!

On my birthday this year
I hope to have a party,
With party poppers, games
And party hats
With lots of fun and cheer!

It's only a couple of weeks to go
Until I will be ten!
I am so very excited
And can't wait until then!

Jessica Lee Bunker (9)
Harrison Primary School, Fareham

Pizza Poem

Cheese, tomato,
Pepperoni too,
Ham and pineapple,
I love you!

Have it for breakfast,
Have it for your lunch,
Have it for your dinner,
Have it for your brunch.

Cook it in the oven,
Cook it on a rock,
But the best way to eat pizza,
Is in your brother's frock!

Elena Gmitrowicz (9)
Harrison Primary School, Fareham

Swimming Lessons

S wimming lessons are so much fun
W hen you get to dive like a dolphin
I nto the warm, wonderful water
M y teacher is called Kelly
M y friends are in my group
I am in the top, which is very deep
N ow I am a very good swimmer
G ood at front crawl and backstroke

L ike an Olympic swimmer
E legantly across the pool
S tarting to get faster
S peeding past my friends
O ver to the other side
N early the end, time to return back to school
S oon enough, you get out ready to get changed again.

Elizabeth Lindsey (10)
Harrison Primary School, Fareham

Rushing Stream

Rushing through our mind,
A stream no one can find,
Flows through the day,
Making us say,
Rushing stream,
It may be a dream,
No one knows rushing stream,
Cutting in on rocks,
Flowing like springboks,
With a bed and no sleep,
Across country it creeps,
Originating from the sky,
Eventually saying goodbye,
As it turns to steam,
Rushing stream.

Connor Jacques-Stevens (10)
Harrison Primary School, Fareham

My Favourite Dinner

When I'm as hungry as a horse
I eat all my favourite dinners, of course

I like curry as hot as fire
Honest I do, I'm not a liar

Tex Mex tortillas, as tasty as can be
I'm a continental eater, can't you see

Piccalilli as yellow as sunshine spread
Bacon sandwiches on fresh white bread

Homemade chicken soup
Mmm! Seconds and thirds please

Discs of pepperoni like flying saucers sitting on my pizza
With all that gooey cheese

Salsa and creamy dips, with vegetable sticks
But in the morning . . . hey, I like my Weetabix

Warm hot chocolate, as cosy as a blanket
I'm off to bed now, looks like I've drank it!

Phoebe Rose-Newton (10)
Harrison Primary School, Fareham

My Dog

My dog is cute
Her name is Sky
I was watching the clouds go by!

I went indoors
And guess what I saw?
Sky and her little claws
And her big bushy tail!
Swish, swish, swish!

Chloe Stoddart (10)
Harrison Primary School, Fareham

The Bat And The Crab

The bat is like a spacecraft ready to abduct its prey
The crab is a tank camouflaged by the night
The bat is like the Devil, bad things blamed on them
The crab is a wonder, everyone looks for them
Which will get the prey first? A juicy worm.
As both of them advance, another is not seen
As it swoops down and takes the worm and flies away
The undangerous sparrow.

Joe Dalby (10)
Harrison Primary School, Fareham

Friends

Good friends will always be there
Good friends will show you they care
Sometimes they are funny
Sometimes they are daft
But when you most need it
They'll always make you laugh.

If you're having problems
She'll always take your side
With her next to you
You'll never need to hide.

At weekends we go shopping
We have lots of fun
We try on lots of clothes
Until we find the one.

We go round each other's houses
For a lovely tea
We chat and play for hours
She's the perfect friend for me.

Kira Carter (10)
Harrison Primary School, Fareham

I, Computer

I want to use my computer,
I can use it as my personal tutor.
I can use it to play many games
And make up lots of funny names.

It helps me do my hard homework
And stops me from going berserk!
It helps me all the time
And helps me find a rhyme.

It shows me loads of awesome pictures,
With lots of photos of brilliant structures!
It holds so many gigabytes
And dazzles me with its flashing lights.

I like to go surfing on the Net,
But not the sites where you can bet.
My favourite website is 123 Spill,
It really gives me a thrill.

I use it to get lots of pictures,
But within P Control strictures.
That P means Parental,
In case you were getting judgemental.

I use it to get obscure rhymes,
Such as fruits like limes.
Or to find a country like Vietnam,
Or a church like Notre Dame.

Off to bed I now must wend,
For sleep should be my friend
And aid my brain to mend
I hope this becomes a trend
But now I must bring this to an end
Cos I'm driving my dad round the bend!

Benedict White (10)
Harrison Primary School, Fareham

Merlin Got Trapped In A Crystal

Merlin got trapped in a crystal,
No one could get him out,
Young King Arthur came along
And said, 'What is going on?'
A young man explained what had happened,
King Arthur said, 'Let me have a go.'

He got his mighty sword called Excalibur
And smashed the crystal with a loud crash,
Merlin fell out and with many thanks,
He gave King Arthur one thousand gold pieces.

That night, Arthur's wife was kidnapped,
No one had seen anything at all,
He went on a search looking everywhere,
But she was nowhere to be found.

King Arthur sent out a telegram,
It read, 'My wife has gone missing,
Whoever is to find her, will be rewarded one thousand gold coins'.
Everyone looked everywhere,
High and low, still no one found her,
King Arthur was desperate,
Looking for his wife.

The next day, he got a letter,
Telling him his wife had been kidnapped,
It also said he must pay ten thousand gold coins,
For them to release his wife.

He would pay them the money,
He would follow them to their base,
He snuck in while no one was looking,
He released his wife and took her back to Camelot.

Alfred Palk (10)
Harrison Primary School, Fareham

Big Yellow Bus

Big yellow bus
You pick me up without any fuss
And take me to school (there is no rush)
I travel on you with all my friends
And when my school day comes to an end
You take me home to my mum again.

Georgia Borrowdale (9)
Harrison Primary School, Fareham

The Gingerbread Man

Quickly, quickly, I've got to run,
I nearly got turned into a ginger bun,
Argh! Look!
There's a very big cook!

Quickly, quickly, I've got to run,
I nearly got turned into a ginger bun,
Argh! Look, there's a dog
And it's got a big log!

Quickly, quickly, I've got to run,
I nearly got turned into a ginger bun,
Wow! Cool! There's a horse
And it's running at gale force.

Quickly, quickly, I've got to run,
I nearly got turned into a ginger bun,
Wicked, cool, wow!
There's a cow!

Quickly, quickly, I've got to run,
I nearly got turned into a ginger bun,
Argh! There's a box,
Next to a hungry fox!

Jake Wheaton (10)
Harrison Primary School, Fareham

The Flightless Bird

In Antarctica, the cold, cold place,
The penguins are slipping, sliding in the snow,
The penguins are attacking a shoal of fish,
They are as fast as lightning, attacking the fish like lions.

When the penguins get out,
They have the catch of the day,
Some rainbow trout, that doesn't taste of sprout,
A bit of plankton to wash it down to get the taste away.

The little penguins frolic and play,
To the bet of the elephant seal lying down at the end of the day,
When they go, they bury deep, deep into the snow,
Tucking themselves into an icy blanket.

Next morning, when they wake, they go fishing
Deep in the ebony ocean,
In the sea, deep in the depths, the penguins play
Amongst the fish,
By evening time a catch of at least twenty each,
But the excitement doesn't end there.

After eating, in the dark, frosty evening,
They go surfing at great, tremendous speeds,
Slipping and sliding
On their tummies, through icy tunnels,
The Emperor penguins shooting through icy funnels.

Morning time and the sun is shining,
Ice glistening all around,
Chicks emerging from their mother's warmth,
Waddling and cheeping and growing fast,
Ready to grow to an adult and start again.

Callum Watson (9)
Harrison Primary School, Fareham

The Allotment

The allotment is very boring,
You weed, pick and sow.
Sometimes there's a hint of fun,
It's nearly all chores though.

In the shed, there's anti-slugs
And killers for the weeds.
Outside there is mouldy veg
And very gone-off peas.

The plants sprout really yucky things,
Like cabbage, onions and leeks.
I wish they could sprout things I like:
Pasta, crisps and sweets.

It has to have its good side too,
There is a bit of fun.
There's toads, slugs and slowworms, *mank!*
And a great big heap of dung!

Daniel McCartney (9)
Harrison Primary School, Fareham

Barbecue

We went to see our friends
I wished it would never end
They had a fantastic swimming pool
And it was very super cool
The barbecue tasted really great
It was the best food I ever ate
With the music we kept dancing
Spinning, hopping, singing, bouncing
When it was late, we went back home
And soon I was in bed alone.

Frank Hussey (10)
Harrison Primary School, Fareham

Mickey And The Pin

There once was a cat called Mickey
Whose owner was called Nicky
Mickey sat on a pin - she looked very grim -
Jumping up, in a spin - Mickey came out
From the house, just as if she was
Chasing a mouse,
We looked for the pin,
But it could not be seen - could it have been
A pussycat dream?

Rebecca Coleborn (9)
Harrison Primary School, Fareham

Being Luke Is Hard!

Being Luke is hard!
Why?

Haircuts, vegetables and baths each day,
Sprouts, pleases and not having my say!
Clothes neatly pressed and bed at eight,
How come Dad gets up so late?

Homework takes priority over telly
And Mum serves up dinner not fit my belly!
My world seems to be falling apart,
But being Luke, is not a bad start!

It's hard being liked, it's hard being good,
I know I'm not quiet and I know that I should,
I'm sure you'll like Luke when he's grown a few years
And over the past, which is a long time, he's had loads of fears.

Luke Bayliss (10)
Harrison Primary School, Fareham

My Room

Sitting on my bed,
Looking all around,
I don't know why it is,
That I can't hear a sound.

When almost every night,
My room begins to speak,
With a gurgle and a groan
And a rather scary creak.

I sit here in the day
And everything is bright,
I try to hear it talk,
But something isn't right.

'It's only all the pipes,' Mum said,
'It's such a lovely place,
It's just four walls, a door and window,
It doesn't have a face.'

So, when I lie in bed tonight
And I'm looking all around,
I shall just look at my precious things
And won't listen to the sound.

Jade Jeffries (10)
Harrison Primary School, Fareham

Smokey Kennings

(In memory of my cat, 28/5/92 - 17/1/06)

Meat muncher
Bone cruncher
Dog fighter
Hard biter
Sharp claws
Big jaws
Fish seizer
Mouse teaser
Fast runner
Crowd stunner
Tree climber
Feline whiner
Rat killer
Cat thriller
Long sleeper
Quiet creeper
Deep digger
Our Tigger
Soft paws
No claws
Soft fur
Contented purr!

Adam Russell Moore (9)
Harrison Primary School, Fareham

Friendship

Friends are important,
Friends can be small,
Friends can be different
And some can be tall,
Some like to run
And some like to crawl.

Friends can be cool,
Friends can be fun,
Friends go to the pool
And some like the sun,
Some like to jump
And some like to hop.

Some friends are really nice
And some friends are mean,
None of them are as quiet as mice
And they never use suncream,
Some friends say nice things,
Some friends just beam.

Hannah Barton (9)
Harrison Primary School, Fareham

Wolves

Sly, fierce wolves
Cold-hearted, mean wolves
Tough, boisterous wolves
Deer-eating, horrid wolves
But there are other wolves like . . .
Canine, loveable wolves
Top dog, mad wolves
Fluffy, likeable wolves
Homesick, crazy wolves.

Emily Shaw (10)
Harrison Primary School, Fareham

Nature

Nature is around me,
Nature is everywhere,
Nature is so beautiful, on the ground and in the air.

Nature is all the flowers,
Nature is all the trees,
Nature is the leaves blowing in the breeze.

Nature is the animals,
That can live in many places,
Nature is the creatures with many different faces.

Nature is growing,
Nature is living,
But then there's a time, when it has to start dying.

Nature is the world,
Nature is my heart,
Nature we should love,
Nature is pure art.

Megan Keri Gamblin (9)
Harrison Primary School, Fareham

The Life Of A Cat

I am a cat, I like to sleep all day
My owners think I am lazy
But they don't see me at night
That's when I go out and play
I enjoy my private life
It certainly is fun all right
And in the morning I get fed
Then it's time for bed.

Jason Hockaday (10)
Harrison Primary School, Fareham

The River And The Sea

As a crocodile slides side to side from left to right
As it snaps on all the fish
As it hits the side of the river
It dives underneath, waiting for its next meal
As some fish swim past, a shark comes along
It opens its huge jaws and crunches
Through the fishes' bones and flesh
As you see the rest of the fish
Go down to the bottom of the deep, dark, blue sea
The rest of the fish look like a skeleton
Dropping from a cliff
As the great white crunches through everything in its way
It meets the fierce crocodile
As the brave great white swims at pace to the crocodile
The crocodile has a bite and they are both never seen again.

George Hoskins (9)
Harrison Primary School, Fareham

Football

I went to a footie match,
To see Portsmouth play,
On their kit there was a patch
Even though they were playing away.

At the end it was 0-0
And went into extra time,
The manager hadn't paid the bill,
So the ball went over the line.

The fans all cheered when Mendez scored,
Even some of the opposing team,
Because they were so bored
And that goal was so mean!

Sam Seymour (10)
Harrison Primary School, Fareham

Chewing Gum

I love chewing gum,
But my mum hates gum,
So does the carpet,
So do the walls,
But I think it rules.

I stick it on my bed,
I even stick it on my head,
As long as I find it,
There's no need to stick,
I really love chewing gum
And I'm not going to forget it.

Everybody hates all the flavours,
But I like cola, mint, banana and all the rest,
My only problem is
I don't know which is best!

Elena Grace Curtis (10)
Harrison Primary School, Fareham

Cats

Oh, what a naughty cat!
Hopping over the walls for snacks,
Scratches your sofas for attention,
Destroys all of your valuables.

Oh, what a good cat!
Kills mice and rats when they are in your house,
Digging a hole for their waste
And they love you as much as you love them.

Cameron Steel (10)
Larmenier & Sacred Heart School, Hammersmith

My Dream

Making my dream, makes me happy
You'll see me swoop and dive and spin and loop
When I live my dream
Dancing in the sky is what I'll do
I'll dance forever, rolling on the clouds
And skipping on the edge of space
That's my dream
Running on air, looking to see how far my dream goes
I guess it's the same as asking how big is the sky
Exploring the sky is my dream, but not on land or sea
But in the airy world itself, in my aeroplane!
An aeroplane that I'm in control of
A real fighter, 'The English Lightning'!
Making my dream *will* make me happy
Especially when I touch the sky!

Liam Foley (11)
Larmenier & Sacred Heart School, Hammersmith

The Weather

The sun comes out to play
The wind wants to blow us away
The snow falls to chill us down
The rain wants to make us run around
The frost in the morning makes us shiver
The fog doesn't help us to get past the river
The lightning strikes and makes noises
The thunder bangs, it sounds like two voices.

Beth Dahlgren (11)
Larmenier & Sacred Heart School, Hammersmith

My Special Jim

(Dedicated to James Maher 1941-2007)

Someone so special
Who lit up my sky
I sat there and wondered
How and why?

How my special person
Could drift by so fast
Watching the days
Go quietly past.

Sat in his bed
In his hospital gown
Feeling awfully tired
And ever so down.

Sharing a smile
And trying to hide
The pain he was keeping
Locked up inside.

Seeing his family
Seeing his friends
Lightened his spirits
Towards the end.

I'll miss his jokes
And big bear hugs
His Cheshire cat grins
And little wry shrugs.

My dear, wonderful
My great, Uncle Jim
Now he's gone
I do miss him.

Rhiannon Evie Maher (11)
Larmenier & Sacred Heart School, Hammersmith

My Fish Bowl

As wet as it can be,
Filled with creatures of the sea.
Trapped in a bowl,
No good for their soul.
They swim round and round,
Not making a sound.

Being fed from time to time,
Not knowing what's going to happen,
Next, there's a child tapping
On the shining glass,
Because it's sitting in a Year 1 class.

Lissy Langtry-Willett (11)
Larmenier & Sacred Heart School, Hammersmith

Games

They are fun
They are enjoyable
In my soup
In my dinner
In my life.
They keep me up at night
They make me change the way I am.
They make me laugh,
They make me cry,
They make me angry
And then I am hungry.
Sometimes boring and sometimes great,
But in general, they are just games.

Brendan Chancusi (10)
Larmenier & Sacred Heart School, Hammersmith

The Best Rapping Cat

The best rapping cat the world has ever seen
Is a slip-slap, tip-tap, clap-clap queen.
She raps in her basket
And up and down the stairs.
She raps in the garden
And raps in and out the chairs.
The best rapping cat, the world has ever seen,
Is a slip-slap, tip-tap, clap-clap queen!

Olivia Campbell (11)
Larmenier & Sacred Heart School, Hammersmith

The Creepy Sounds

The trees go *swish*
All the doors go *bang*
The thunder goes *crack*
And the wind goes *woo*
The lights go on and off
The rain goes *drip, drip, drip*
The windows go *smash*
I'm in a big storm.

Reina Miguens-Souto (9)
Larmenier & Sacred Heart School, Hammersmith

Bunny

I've got a little bunny,
He cost a lot of money,
He is very funny
And he likes to play when it's sunny.

He likes to eat grass,
He is very fast,
I love him very much
And he lives in a hutch.

Matilda Cook (9)
Larmenier & Sacred Heart School, Hammersmith

Skyluck

Skyluck was a cargo ship,
It saved thousands of people,
During the Vietnam War.
Skyluck sailed for eight whole months,
The only good thing to eat were baked beans.
But on the last day,
All they could eat was flour mixed with water.

Eventually the ship reached land
And passing people took pity and gave change,
To those people in rags.
My dad got a job
And he met my mum,
They got married,
I was born
And this is how it all happened.

Patrick Huynh (10)
Larmenier & Sacred Heart School, Hammersmith

My Little Brother

My brother's name is Patrick
He is only five
He is a very good swimmer
And really likes to dive
Patrick loves football too
He wears a Chelsea shirt
But plays at Craven Cottage
I worry in case he gets hurt
Patrick likes to play
Power Rangers are his favourite toy
We sometimes play together
He is a lovely boy.

Elizabeth Farrell (8)
Larmenier & Sacred Heart School, Hammersmith

Family

Your family will always be there for you,
When you're feeling low or angry too.
When you're just a kid, you feel
That life is a nightmare and you are
Forever saying that it isn't fair.
As you grow older you start to realise
Not to take things for granted
And to sometimes just step aside
Your brothers and sisters sometimes fight
In the early hours of the morning
Or darkness of the night
At the end of the day, it all comes down to one thing
That if you feel sad or low
Just give your family a ring.

Lauren O'Driscoll (11)
Larmenier & Sacred Heart School, Hammersmith

Flying In The Sky

If I could fly up and through the sky
In a plane just as high as the stars, moon and sun
That would be such good fun
Flying through the clouds
Watching the sunset like a ball of fire
I can feel the wind on my face as I glide
I have freedom with wings on my side.

George Oppe (10)
Larmenier & Sacred Heart School, Hammersmith

The Sun

The sun that shines so bright in the morning
The sun that shines so bright in the evening
The sun that shines so bright in the day
The sun that shines so bright in every way.

Banna Hannes
Larmenier & Sacred Heart School, Hammersmith

Her Feelings . . . Love

She never felt that way,
She never knew one day,
She would feel that way,
She held his hand,
As a really good friend.

Her feelings changed,
From friendship to love,
She never thought the friendship would
Become something special,
Something that can be really stressful.

He knew that the way
She looked at him changed,
But he didn't know
What she had in mind,
Or deep in the inside.

She kept her secret to herself,
But as she kept her feelings,
Times passed,
So she was left behind by him,
And for the rest of her life,
Her love was never alive.

Bruna Baltazar Prates (10)
Larmenier & Sacred Heart School, Hammersmith

Spring

In spring flowers open,
Shooting from the ground,
From blossoms to daffodils,
Their brightly coloured patterns,
Point to infinity and beyond.

Carolanne Cannon (10)
Larmenier & Sacred Heart School, Hammersmith

The Little Boy Who Was A Chimney Sweep

There once was a small and unhappy boy,
Who climbed up the chimney and swept,
His skinny body and short, weak bones,
Climbed up and up and up,
Whilst his knees and elbows bled painfully
He very quietly wept.

In and under his eyes
Was very dark black soot,
Which he wiped with his torn and shabby clothes,
Up in that chimney, he cried the soot out
And wished his eyes could be closed.

The soot he breathed in from the chimney,
Had a horrible scent,
There he died in the chimney
And down the sweeping broom went.

Grace Galbraith (10)
Larmenier & Sacred Heart School, Hammersmith

A Poem Celebrating The Abolition Of Slavery

I have just been set free,
I can feel a gentle breeze,
I look forward to what awaits me,
I can see the blinding light,
From the warm, heating sun.

The birds are singing with joy,
Now the time has come,
I am running in the sun,
With a happy smile on my face.

Shannon Morrissey (9)
Larmenier & Sacred Heart School, Hammersmith

Me

I have two legs.
I have two arms.
I have five fingers on each hand.
I have five toes on each foot.
I have one head.
I have two eyebrows.
I have one mouth.
I have one tummy.
That's what makes me,
                    Me!

Andy Williams (11)
Larmenier & Sacred Heart School, Hammersmith

Chocolate

Chocolate, chocolate, melts in my mouth
Chocolate, chocolate, you taste so good
Chocolate, chocolate, please don't go
Chocolate, chocolate, you're so scrumptious
Chocolate, chocolate, I want a bite.

Abigail Barber (9)
Larmenier & Sacred Heart School, Hammersmith

Dragon, Dragon

The dragon swoops, the dragon soars,
I see the dragon, but now no more,
His wings have the moonlight shining, shining,
He flies through the dark black sky,
All you see is the moon and the dragon,
Then it's gone, gone, gone forever.

Lettice Gatacre (10)
Larmenier & Sacred Heart School, Hammersmith

Slavery

The chilly winter
Comes again
Crunch, crunch
Under my feet
Building snowmen
Having fights
Tickly snowflakes
Fall to my feet.

I am on a big wooden ship
I can't even remember my name
My mum is selling children for money
And my dad is really sick
These big, fat men are around me
Teasing me and waking me
With a big metal hammer
I want to go back to my family
I'm only a little boy
My best friend is begging.

Olivia Hardy (9)
Larmenier & Sacred Heart School, Hammersmith

Cheeky

C heeky monkey, cheeky monkey
H ow are you
E very day I think of you and the fun we used to have
E very time you made me feel so happy and so sad
K ind, cheeky monkey, lovely cheeky monkey
Y ou will always be my friend.

Aeysha Robinson (9)
Larmenier & Sacred Heart School, Hammersmith

Nature Is Calling

Nature is calling,
Calling in my ears,
Next minute, I saw a little bird,
Tweeting in the air.

Nature is calling,
Calling in my nose,
Suddenly, I made a sneeze,
Then smelt a little flower
Swaying in the breeze.

Nature is calling,
Calling in my eyes,
I chanced to spy a butterfly,
What a beautiful surprise.

Nature is calling,
Calling in my hair,
Even though I can't see it,
The wind is blowing everywhere.

Nature is calling,
Calling on my tongue,
I see those red, rosy apples,
Dangling on the tree,
Urging me to come.

Lucy Rhiemus (9)
Larmenier & Sacred Heart School, Hammersmith

Storm

S torm crashed and smashed at the door
T errifying children through the night
O nly Daddy loudly snores
R ain made him sleep even more tight
M ummy will come and we will be alright.

Samuel McHugh (8)
Larmenier & Sacred Heart School, Hammersmith

The March Of Time

I stood on a hill
And watched the march of time go by
This didn't really happen
It was in my mind's eye.

Leading the way on his black horse
Was Attila the Hun
His men on foot behind him
Simply had to run.

Then came some chariots
Driven by Romans
After that some horses
Ridden by Normans.

Next, came some Vikings
Strong as boulders
Carrying their long ship
On their shoulders.

Following the long boat
Strolled King Henry the Cut Throat.

Then came the Saxons
In wooden carts
Alongside some Celts
Who stopped for a game of darts.

At the end of the line
Was a knight in armour
And he waved to me
As he rode his llama!

Cormac Auty (8)
Larmenier & Sacred Heart School, Hammersmith

Dogs

Dogs make a lot of noise,
Whilst chewing on their favourite toys,
Dogs always like running in the park,
Until it gets dark,
Dogs like to run, run, run,
Until they get tired after having so much fun.

When that dog finally sleeps,
Boy, wouldn't you get a lot of peace,
When that dog finally wakes up,
Please don't make him start to bark,
Why not just take him to the park,
Where he could get tired,
Before it gets dark!

Darnell Thomas (11)
Larmenier & Sacred Heart School, Hammersmith

Silence

As I stand on the path of the silent park,
I see people's mouths moving, but no sound emerging,
The dog panting by, but no sound of his paw,
The joy and happiness coming from the children,
But I can't hear,
The blazing sun beaming
With its yellow rays, nothing heard,
Bumping and banging coming from the basketball,
Birds crossing by in the high blue sky
And not even the sound of the lawn mower
Is to be heard.

Lauryn Pierro (9)
Larmenier & Sacred Heart School, Hammersmith

The Beautiful Silence

I sit in the comfort of my warm bed,
Staring out at the moonlight,
The beautiful silence enveloping the world.
Its rich blue colour, spreading out,
Like an old man reaching for his stick.
Sounds like a dark ripple, engulfing the silent, cold lake
In lonely surroundings, jumping with excited fish.
Not even a rat in the beautiful moonlight,
Scowling for prey after escape from a vicious kitten.
It tastes like a soft drop of rain reaching down
Towards a quiet street from the thunderous clouds above.
Smells like freezing air wafting its way
Around the icy mountains of Antarctica.
It all reminds me of a lonely snowman waiting patiently
In a snowy field, for an orange carrot nose.
All in the beautiful moonlight, right out of my window.

George Hanoun (10)
Larmenier & Sacred Heart School, Hammersmith

Silence

As I cross the enchanted stream
Not a ripple in the water, not a rustle in the trees
It sounds as quiet as a baby sleeping without a sound
A hare stops in the moonlight, as still and as quiet as can be
Not a crack, nor a thump, nothing at all
Silence is white, plain and nothing more
As I come to the end of the bridge, I fall into darkness
No more moonlight, I'm just alone with the trees
Suddenly, the bridge disappeared, how will I get home?
Oh, I'm alone with the trees.

Molly Spring (10)
Larmenier & Sacred Heart School, Hammersmith

Death

Today I died,
Shivers ran down my spine
Blood freezing like you are in the North Pole, lying in the snow,
Lying in my grave,
Not knowing what to do next,
At night I hear crows shouting
Kill, kill, kill.
Hearing wolves howling to the moon,
Pitch-black, cannot see light,
Like in a dark cave with only a candle to see,
Suddenly, I hear a voice calling my name
And saying, 'Nima, Nima, follow the light.'
Not knowing who it is, then I see bright gold gates
I now know what it is, *Heaven!*
I smile and say, 'What happened?
God says, 'You're dead!'

Nima Oscar Pourdad (10)
Larmenier & Sacred Heart School, Hammersmith

Anger

Anger is like a red-hot pot of soup
Just waiting to explode
Smells like a burnt building breaking apart
Feels like a hot iron
Noisy like a steaming hot kettle boiling
Fast like a Ferrari on the road
Looks like a big blob of blood on a knee
Tastes like a spicy hot piece of curry.

Chizi Amadi (10)
Larmenier & Sacred Heart School, Hammersmith

Rugby Crazy

Sunday is here, my favourite day
Rugby, my passion, has to be played!
I put on my club kit
Eager, excited and fit
And I'm driven by Dad
To meet up with the lads.

Out on the playing field
I tackle like I'm wearing a shield
Determined and fearless, I go at them
No points to be given, I must defend
The opponents are strong, but just can't run
We win so easily and have such fun!

Joe Stapleton (9)
Larmenier & Sacred Heart School, Hammersmith

My Grandma

I looked at my grandma and what did I see?
A beautiful face looking at me.

I looked at my grandma and what did I see?
A tongue that was longer than me.

I looked at my grandma and what did I see?
A thick little belly rumbling like jelly.

I looked at my grandma and what did she see?
A little boy staring back at she.

Luca Nicolaou (8)
Larmenier & Sacred Heart School, Hammersmith

History

History is history
It's what's happened in the past
History is history
Who's starring in the cast?

The leading man is Henry VIII
His wife, well, heaven knows!
He worked his way through six of them
Henry kept them on their toes.

The supporting role is Cromwell
Who wasn't a nice chap,
He had Charles the first beheaded
The head fell in his lap!

History is history
Who knows what happens next?
History is history
Will you be in the text?

Joseph McWeeney (8)
Larmenier & Sacred Heart School, Hammersmith

Monkeys

Monkeys, monkeys, were in the air,
Monkeys, monkeys, were in the lair,
Monkeys, monkeys, were everywhere,
But the humans didn't care.

So they cut the forest as if it were their hair,
Soon it was monkeys, monkeys are not in the air,
Monkeys, monkeys, aren't in the lair,
Monkeys, monkeys, are now nowhere
And it's so not fair!

Mark Farag (11)
Larmenier & Sacred Heart School, Hammersmith

Holiday

When the moon is shining
And it's nice and bright
I like to walk the beach at night
To see the stars up in the sky
I sometimes wish that I could fly.
I love to hear the sea go swish
And throw a coin in to make a wish
In the morning when the sun is rising
This day could be as surprising
To sit on the beach or go for a swim
We just don't know how to begin
So when we are on holiday
Nothing really matters
We can sing, dance, laugh and swim
And act as mad as hatters!

Rebecca Hare (9)
Larmenier & Sacred Heart School, Hammersmith

Going Up The Tree

We're going up, up, up the tree
So as not to wake the bee
Then down, down, down we go
Oh, we are so very low

We're going up and down the tree
Here goes Joe, Beth, Rick and Frannie
Up and down, up and down
Now let's get a pound

Louise, Maddy and Marie
Are going up the tree.

Louise De Thomasson (9)
Larmenier & Sacred Heart School, Hammersmith

Your Best Friend

Kings and queens of this land
Always have a friendly dog close at hand
So when you are lonely, scared and sad
Get a dog and life won't be so bad
If you want a dog, ask permission
Or it will be a futile mission
Dogs are expensive, big or small
They need a lot of exercise and a good ball
They'll rip up your house, they'll rip up your shoes
They may even rip up your daily news
Dogs need plenty of exercise and care
Dogs are for life, so beware
Dogs are fun
Throw a ball and they will run
As the sun rises, they're up and ready to play
As the sun sets, they're down and ready to lay
If dogs could talk, I'm sure that they would say
With a great, big yawn and a stretch, 'Another fine day!'

Kristina Novakovic (8)
Larmenier & Sacred Heart School, Hammersmith

The Sun

The sun shining really bright,
It is a really hot star,
It stands there as the Earth moves around it,
The sun is boiling, blaring out light,
Yet it always appears to come down at night.

The Earth's heat comes from the sun,
The flaring flames send heatwaves,
The summer is when the sun gets boiling,
Soon the sun will not give light,
So the Earth won't be bright.

Thomas Whear (10)
Larmenier & Sacred Heart School, Hammersmith

Space

Space is dark and dull,
But stars and moon,
Light it all up,
First comes Mercury, very, very hot,
Next comes Venus, it has acid clouds,
After, comes Earth, exactly where we live,
Now comes Mars, quite close to Earth,
Then comes Jupiter, bigger than Earth,
Soon comes Saturn, it could float on water,
Now comes Uranus, made of gas and liquid
And now comes Neptune, with the great dark spot,
The last planet is . . . Pluto, very, very small.

Caroline Babisz (10)
Larmenier & Sacred Heart School, Hammersmith

I Wish I Could Fly

I wish I could fly
Way up in the sky
It would be so fun
I could watch the sun

I would fly around
Fly up and down
I would fly so high
Straight into the sky

I'm not scared of flying
I really am not lying
Take me up in the air
And meet me up there.

Sophie Castillo (9)
Larmenier & Sacred Heart School, Hammersmith

Horses

H orses run wild
O ver the hills and mountains
R unning, galloping, cantering and trotting
S hires are the horse giants
E ver so tall, never too small
S o many horses all around, Shetlands, Shires lead the ground.

Ellee Thomas & Nova Olympia Dora (10)
Larmenier & Sacred Heart School, Hammersmith

Spring

Blossoms blooming
Sun shining
That's the life of spring
T-shirts and shorts
That's what we're wearing
New young animals
Lambs and chicks
Drinking lots
Licking lots of ice cream
That's the life of spring.

Beth Hayes (9)
Larmenier & Sacred Heart School, Hammersmith

The Dog

The dog is lively and loves to play
He jumps and pounces all day
And all night he curls up beside me just like a ball
The next day the dog wakes up and goes downstairs
And plays with its squeaky toy, *squeak, squeak, squeak*
The dog plays with me and jumps up at me
The dog is cute and fluffy, fluffy, fluffy
That dog is mine
The dog is mine.

Amie Murray (9)
Larmenier & Sacred Heart School, Hammersmith

The Train

The train roars loudly, as he puffs out of the tunnel,
Like a dragon coming out of its lair,
The steam forms enchanting shapes, as it comes out of the funnel,
Like in a dream,
The dragon whistles a loud, angry tune,
Deafening every living creature,
He rests in the night, under the moon,
Snoring loudly, ready to work the next day.

Natalia Watrobska (10)
Larmenier & Sacred Heart School, Hammersmith

Back In The Daze

Back in the days when the sky was clearer . . .
Back in them days when the sun shined brighter . . .
Back in the days every citizen was its own fighter . . .
Back in the days when God was the first teacher . . .
Back in the days when the streets were smaller . . .
Back in the days when I thought my life was slower . . .
Back in the days when everyone was a gangster . . .
Back in the days when all the children in the neighbourhood
Were all a lot smarter
Now we find today's kids are growing and growing
Until they're 7.5 feet tall, but they're still getting dumber . . .
And there's nothing the parents can do
Because they're plane dumb too . . .
So they're growing and growing
Until you don't think they'll stop
But they're dumber than ever
When will they be clever?
I think that's
Never
Or maybe not . . .

Lulu Anthonia Olokun (10)
Larmenier & Sacred Heart School, Hammersmith

WWII

(Marian Hoedt died November 2003 - he was my grandfather)

I'm 18 and my name is Marian Hoedt
I can only bring injured to the medic tents
I could get shot
I could walk on a landmine.

The soldiers caught me
They arrested me
And took me to a concentration camp
All I can do is wait.

It's been a long time
Argh!
I just got shot in the chest
It was a drunk Nazi guard.

I met a lady today, her name I do not know
She is beautiful
She is from the other side of Poland
She was captured too for helping the injured.

It is 2003 now, 60 odd years since the war finished
The lady I met in the war, I married
She died in 1993
I feel I'm going to die soon
But you never know.

Leandros Philiotis (10)
Larmenier & Sacred Heart School, Hammersmith

Shark

S harks swim in the open sea
H ave got sharp teeth
A nd fins which poke out of the sea
R ushing towards animals
K illing them in one bite.

Patrick McCoy (10)
Larmenier & Sacred Heart School, Hammersmith

WWII - My Great Grandad

Why do we have to have this foolish war?
The Führer and his men are just asking for more.

My great grandad was nearly the highest rank
He got shot in the leg by a tiger tank.

He thought his life was over then
Luckily he was saved by his men.

My great grandad survived the whole of the war
Other people were lying dead on the floor.

Daniel Lord (10)
Larmenier & Sacred Heart School, Hammersmith

Cheetah

Cheetahs are as fast as the wind
They have got long legs
Cheetahs eat meat night and day
They lay down and go to sleep.

The war is when people fight
And it is a really big fright
And people shoot their guns
At each other every day.

The sun is a round ball
Like a sphere it is
A burning ball of fire
And it can kill you.

Max Spiers (10)
Larmenier & Sacred Heart School, Hammersmith

Space

The magnificent planets
Hang in mid air
As stars light up
The immeasurable universe.

Shooting stars
Race rockets
In the pitch-black sky
As comets crash across our galaxy.

Why is it so big?
Why are we so small?

Lottie Longfellow (10)
Larmenier & Sacred Heart School, Hammersmith

Cars

I like fast cars
Loud and noisy.

I like new cars
Shiny and bright.

I like big cars
Engines loud.

If I could drive a car
A Ferrari it would be.

Lewis Hobbs (8)
Littledown Special Needs School, Slough

Spider-Man

Spider-Man can climb
High and low.
He saves peoples lives
He's a superhero.
I would be Spider-Man
If only I could.
Because I am brave
And good.

Dominic Czerny Ward (7)
Littledown Special Needs School, Slough

Homework

I'm worried about my homework,
I don't know what to do,
My teachers won't let me shirk,
Can you help me too?

The drawing bit is easy
I'm puzzled about the rest,
Oh, I'm worried about my homework,
I'm really very stressed!

Problems aren't so easy,
The English is hard as well,
The geography is a mission to workout,
I really cannot tell!

This homework is impossible,
I can't do it all,
I need to finish my homework,
Before the end of school!

Emma-Rose Reynolds (10)
St Hilary's School, Godalming

Swallows

I love swallows,
I don't know why,
They come to my house,
Where do they go?
Where do they fly?

Do they go and bask in the sun?
Do they go and have lots of fun?
Do they go somewhere colder
Or do they go somewhere so hot, they smoulder?

Do they go to outer space,
Or some other rather strange place?
If I was a swallow, I know what I'd do,
I wouldn't want to go away and fly.

If I was a swallow,
I'd rather stay in my home,
Because I wouldn't want
To leave it all alone.

Anna Timms (10)
St Hilary's School, Godalming

Flowers

F lowers are beautiful
L aying in the sun
O verlooking the lush, green grass
W aving their leaves up and down
E xpertly spreading their petals
R eaching for the sky
S waying in the wind, *swish, swish!*

Sophie Figueiredo (9)
St Hilary's School, Godalming

Mog's Menu

I have a dog whose name is Mog,
I love him with all my heart,
I give him lots of treats to eat
And this is how it starts:
On Monday he scoffed down some ham,
On Tuesday he gobbled some roast lamb,
On Wednesday he had sweets,
On Thursday he ate mustard,
On Friday he had seconds of custard,
On Saturday I gave him kippers
And to repay me for my love and kindness,
On Sunday, he ate my slippers!

Hayley Foster (8)
St Hilary's School, Godalming

The Penguin

Penguin swims down south
And catches fish in his mouth,
On the ice he slides,
Into the water he glides,
What's that he spies
With his eagle eyes?
He must be speedy,
For his family is greedy,
The sea otters want their share,
As is only fair,
But as he sleeps at night,
In a huddle on the ice,
He dreams of the fun,
He could have in the sun!

Kitty Briggs (9)
St Hilary's School, Godalming

Funfair Senses

Glittering machines which light up in the sky,
The Hall of Mirrors; looking silly!
Pony rides for the first time,
The fiery brightness blinding you in the eye.

People eating candyfloss, which is delicious!
They also eat hotdogs and ice cream,
I love it when Mum buys me chips!
There are a large variety of sweets!

The loud music is so strong and ear-splitting,
Screams of people on the ghost train!
The fast food sellers are shouting, 'Food!'
The talk of the people wanting to go on rides.

The scent of the hotdogs is so strong,
I can't help myself from having one!
I really love fast food; my mum says it's bad for me,
I can smell ice cream a mile away!
Candyfloss gives a very strong scent!

The smooth dodgem cars are a lovely thing to feel,
The handles of the horses on the merry-go-round
Are lovely to feel too,
The bars to keep you safe on big rides feel safe,
The feel of candyfloss melting on my tongue at the end of the day
When it's time to go home.

Rosie Jameson (9)
St Hilary's School, Godalming

Funfair Senses

Hear . . .

Screams of children on the rides
Clattering and crashing of the dodgems
Jokes and laughter heard in the crowd
Stall-holders shouting to families.

Feel . . .

An evening breeze blowing gently
Lots of soft toys to win
The lovely grass below you
A hard, hairy coconut waits to be hit.

Taste . . .

Irresistible ice cream on the stalls
Big, fat hamburgers too tempting to resist
Lovely, cool lemonade which is so fizzy
Sweet, fluffy candyfloss hanging up from rails.

See . . .

Lots of clowns walking on stilts
Fantastic games going on everywhere
Little tiny lights glowing all around
Scary rides making people sick and green.

Smell . . .

Fumes from cars wafting around
Lots of smelly animals in their pens
Strong perfume coming from the ladies
Tasty food at the small stalls.

Megan Lavan (9)
St Hilary's School, Godalming

Flowers

Emerald-green leaves shining in the sun,
Leaves swaying in the breeze,
As green as new grass,
Leaves like soft feathers,
Leaves like rough stones.

The colours are as bright as a rainbow,
Forget-me-not-blue,
Azalea purple and daffodil-yellow,
Rose-pink tulips bright in the sun,
The flash of colours, like
Yellow, orange, red, purple and cream.

The petals of the flowers are perfectly coloured,
Like paper in the wind,
So soft to touch,
Some so sharp to feel,
The beautiful scented smell fills the air.

Sophie Johnson (9)
St Hilary's School, Godalming

Snowflakes

Snowflakes are cold, icy and frosty,
They have unique designs and are beautiful,
Snowflakes can be tasty and thin,
They are light, soft and feathery,
Snowflakes can be sparkly white or gleaming wet,
They are fragile!
If you touch one, it will melt,
You cannot see them,
Usually they are tiny,
Some of them are see-through
And most of them are white,
They are frozen water!

Elizabeth Coughlan (9)
St Hilary's School, Godalming

The Garden

The garden has a little sparkling waterfall
And long grass which goes up to your hips,
The flower beds are covered in flowers,
In all sorts of colours and shapes,
One big oak tree stood at the back of the garden,
Easy to climb it was,
I sat there staring out of my window,
At our garden.

Sophie Turner (8)
St Hilary's School, Godalming

Funfair Senses

Colourful, dazzling lights
Fun, enjoyable pony rides
Happy, excited people waiting at the rides
Scary, haunted ghost trains.

Sticky, white candyfloss sticks
Hard, hairy tennis balls being thrown
Warm, milky, tasty coconuts being taken away
Wonderful, pleasing coins and notes in your hands.

Mouth-watering, tempting and delicious hot dogs
Pink bubbles exploding in your mouth
Tasty vanilla and strawberry ice cream
Sweet, raspberry, sticky candyfloss.

Sizzling, burning and nice-smelling burgers
Smoky bacon streaks cooking at a stall
Salty chips and watery cod in a bag
Smelly and delicious hotdogs.

Screaming, hysterical laughter
Noisy, crashing and clattering of the dodgem cars
Happy, excited, friendly voices
Persuading sounds from the people at the stalls.

Rebecca Johnson (9)
St Hilary's School, Godalming

Dark

'I don't like the dark, Mum,'
'I don't like the dark, Mum,'
'That's all I hear from my daughter Gemma.'
She moans and complains
And thinks I'm insane
To like the dark.

'I don't like the dark, Mum,'
I used to say when I was five
And my mum used to come upstairs
With sleepy dust in her eyes,
She'd tell me such delightful things
I would sleep that night
And the next evening when I was in bed I said,
'Mummy, please turn out the light.'

Georgina Cave (10)
St Hilary's School, Godalming

The Nightmare

I sit in my bed, listening to the wind,
Rattling and swirling outside,
I dare to get out of bed . . .
I hear the wind whining in the keyhole,
The old oak tree creaking in the night.

I imagine vampires waking up from their slumber,
The moon shining like marble,
I toss and turn in my bed,
I try to get to sleep, but I can't,
I imagine witches making potions in bubbling cauldrons.

Suddenly, I see the tree's branches
Turning into fingers, then black!
I wake up in the morning,
Phew!

Madeleine Clench (9)
St Hilary's School, Godalming

Can I Get A Mouse?

'Mum, can I get a mouse?'
'No way,
Not in this house.'
'I could call it Fay,
They are born in May,
That's next month,
There are black ones,
Blue ones,
Brown ones
And albino ones.'
'No!
The hounds are bound to chase it.'
'Please?
It won't run about on the ground,
I will have a cage,
Please,
They don't make much sound,
Please . . . ?'

'Oh, fine!'

Ellie Richardson (9)
St Hilary's School, Godalming

Stars

In the night, a star competition starts,
Lots of shouts come from the other stars,
Music comes flowing in from the star band.

Stars twinkle and shine,
Like they are the star of the show,
They glisten and gleam,
Like they are the only ones which glow,
But when the moon comes out,
It all changes for the stars,
They're not the ones that get first prize,
But they still try next year!

Charlotte Coxon (9)
St Hilary's School, Godalming

I Can't Do That

I can't do that,
Sweeping the floor,
Tidying my room,
You can do that if you want,
But I can't do that.

I can't do that,
My maths homework, it's too hard,
Feeding my brother,
Washing the toilet,
It's horrible and smelly, oh Mum,
I can't do that.

I can't do that,
Cleaning the windows,
Washing the bath, oh Dad, help me,
I can't do that.

I can do this,
I can brush my hair
And get dressed,
Yes, Mum, I can definitely do that!

Jess Crathern (9)
St Hilary's School, Godalming

I Am Desperate

I am desperate,
For a fountain pen
To write with
In my class.

I am desperate,
For my ears pierced,
To show off,
To all my friends.

I am desperate,
For a pet hamster,
I'll do my very best,
At everything you ask me,
I'll even wear a vest!

I am desperate,
For my dad back,
He helped me through my troubles,
Dad, where are you now?

Dad, I love you,
Goodnight.

Sophie Bokor-Ingram (9)
St Hilary's School, Godalming

Hair

Hair is great,
If you want it long, you'll have to wait,
Hair can be unfair,
It makes me despair,
Gets nits and terrible bits.

It makes me hot,
Unless I get it wet,
My mum ties it up into a towel-like net,
But that never works,
So I put up with it.

But now it's nice,
So I can sit back with a glass of ice,
It has been cut,
So it's neat,
I'm not so hot,
It lets out heat!

Kayleigh Berry (9)
St Hilary's School, Godalming

Cheeky Monkey

I came home from school
And found that a monkey
Was sitting on my stool,
He ate all the bananas, pears and plums
Then I shouted, 'Mum!'
When he left, I found out he was a thief,
I called the police and said
I had a thief who ate all my bananas, pears and plums,
The very next day, in the month of May,
I saw him again and told him to stay away!

Hannah Kearns (9)
St Hilary's School, Godalming

My Only Cat!

My gorgeous cat,
Sits on her red, rough mat
And sleeps there all day long.

She only wakes up,
At 12 o'clock
And that's definitely wrong!

She has a friend,
That lives round the bend,
Who is named Pat,
That swallowed a bat!

My puffed up cat,
Is very, very fat,
Who is such a nasty brat,
That is still, my precious cat.

Aminah Aleem (10)
St Mark's Junior School, Southampton

Naughty Sam

Under the table
Is naughty Sam,
His hands are all sticky
From eating the jam.

Looking around
Sam quickly jumps out,
His face is all sticky
He hears Mum shout!

Looking around at all the mess,
Under the table, Mum spots the jam!
She has an idea who it might be,
So Mum yells, *'Sam!'*

Florence Blatchford (9)
St Mark's Junior School, Southampton

An Eeyore Poem

Little donkey, Eeyore
Was out one day,
Over the hills
And far away.

Pooh and Tigger said,
'Please come back.'
So little donkey, Eeyore
Came plodding with a sack.

Eeyore went off
With his friends one day
And all of them went
To go and play.

Piglet, Rabbit and Roo
Came to play
Over the hills
And far away.

Gina England (10)
St Mark's Junior School, Southampton

Missing You

I hide my tears,
When I say your name,
But the pain in my heart,
Is still the same.
Although I smile
And seem carefree,
There is no one who misses you
More than me!
I love you so much,
You mean the world to me
And I can't imagine my life without you
Anymore.

Jagjit Singh Potiwal (10)
St Mark's Junior School, Southampton

Sensing A Performance

I watch the dancer before me performing
And I hear the audience whispering their praise
Hairspray fills my nostrils and makes me want to sneeze
Licking my lips, I taste the red lipstick painting a smile on my face
My fingers clutch my silky costume, nervously.

The stage blacks out and the lights go on,
My music starts, then I am gone.

Bethany Drouêt-Lewis (10)
St Mark's Junior School, Southampton

The Seaside

We pack and race to the car
With no petrol
We don't get very far!

Dad runs in a hurry
And gets a supply of petrol
So we don't need to worry!

We finally arrive at the beach
The clouds above
Seem just out of reach.

We start to play and have fun
Ice creams are eaten
And we start to run.

The day comes to an end
We've made friends that are cool
I say goodbye to my one and only friend.

Lauren Gibbens (10)
St Mark's Junior School, Southampton

ınnel

ɔss,
love,
brings,
above.

Тᴴᴇ▪ ɪore laughter,
No more fun,
It's quiet and lonely,
Their happiness is done.

You sit, heartbroken,
All alone,
Empty, unfilled,
All of it gets shown.

Your eyes fill with tears,
Your joyfulness forever gone,
Your life torn in shreds,
Missing your loved one's song.

Your smile faded,
In the darkness,
The tunnel, coal-black,
Full of your sadness.

Cala Ricketts (10)
St Mark's Junior School, Southampton

My Sister

Little, short hair,
A little button nose,
Her cheeks are so pink,
Like a lovely, beautiful rose.

She is so very annoying,
But very, very sweet,
I also have to keep an eye on her
And I hate the way she eats.

She has one big sister
And that is obviously me,
Most of the time she is quiet,
But she can be buzzy like a bumblebee.

Did I mention that her name is Lilly?
Well, she is five years old,
She is very mean for her age
And never gets told.

So, that was my poem,
That's all I've got to say,
Oh, there is one more thing,
Would you like to meet her one day?

Hannah Rapley (9)
St Mark's Junior School, Southampton

The Brave Soldier

My brave soldier
Is seven foot three
He's the strongest soldier
You'll ever see.

He fights dragons
Sea serpents
Three-headed dogs
Even gigantic, poisonous bugs.

He does any quest
You ask him to do
From slaying a dragon
To stealing gold from a wagon.

He wears a helmet
Armour, shield and sword
He does anything
He never gets bored.

Ahmad Akbari (10)
St Mark's Junior School, Southampton

The Calm Sea

The stunning sea is so relaxing,
The calm and silky sea is so huge,
Whoosh!
I hear the water splash,
It looks splendid!

The water is crashing with the waves,
I feel so sleepy,
The water is as majestic
As the Royal Queen.

Sabina Akter-Kamali (10)
St Paul with St Luke Primary School, Bow

The Calm And Rough Sea!

The sea is amazing and calm
Doesn't want to cause any harm
It's smooth, soft, gentle and silky
Sometimes, people say it's nice and milky.

The sea is always shining
When it's moving from side to side
Everyone thinks it's stunning.

The sea opens at the mouth
So loud that anything can hear it
Even a mouse
Even from its own house
Splash! Swish! Slam! On the rocks.

The sea is strong, as wild as bulls
Crashing and bashing on the walls
Crunching and munching everything in its way
Dashing around wherever it may.

The sea is as fast as a cheetah
The sea is even furious that anyone can be
The sea is older than the life in me.

Jamilur Rahman (10)
St Paul with St Luke Primary School, Bow

The Calm Sea!

The calm sea shimmering in my eyes
I hear the water go *whoosh!*
Then I see the water push, coming to me!
Water is as silky as a smooth, shiny snake
I relax and sleep while the water is bubbling
The sea is as clean as pure water
I listen to the sea and I fall asleep.

Aniqa Ferdaus (9)
St Paul with St Luke Primary School, Bow

Angel Sea

I am a calm sea
And I start off like this . . .

First, I am a stream
Rolling down the mountain's eyes,
That's not really a surprise,
Splish, splash, splosh!

I join another river,
That leads into a fall,
Rushing down another hill,
Listening to people call,
Whoosh!

Now a rapid is controlling me,
I am near a waterfall,
Oh no!
I am going to crash into a wall!
Down I go! *Splash!*

Yes! I made it down to the calming sea,
Now I'm very shallow,
People want to paddle in me
And that is why I am simply called,
The calming angel sea!

Rochelle Jethoo (10)
St Paul with St Luke Primary School, Bow

The Calm Death

Going down the river, *splash, whoosh*
That you may never, ever
Think that you're there
You may never be a river
You may think that you're dreaming
But you never will be
On the calm river
Heading for the grimy green river
Could never, ever be true.

Jabir Ahmed (10)
St Paul with St Luke Primary School, Bow

The Chocolate River

The calm, soft, shiny waterfall
Falling gently into the
Beautiful, silky river
The lovely children
Splishing, splashing
Into the calm, soft river
The hot, fuzzy river
Flowing through the country
The chocolate river is there
For you to chill and enjoy
Have a break and relax in the river
That's why I'm called the chocolate river.

Sadia Sharmin Ahmed (10)
St Paul with St Luke Primary School, Bow

Travelling Sea

I'm swaying as smooth as leaves,
Travelling from here to Australia,
Whoosh! As I travel to the Outback,
Dolphins spring out of me, like bouncing balls.

Swish as I heat boats,
Rocking like a baby's cradle,
As I am nearly there,
Ssh! I come to the edge of the beach,
As calm as babies sleeping.

Whoosh! As I go back.

James Marling (10)
St Paul with St Luke Primary School, Bow

The Calm Death

I am travelling calmly
As I go, people chuck stones at me
I get furious
Now I go at sonic speed
As I fall from a wonderful waterfall
Nothing can stop me
I will defeat anything that stands in my way
Splish, splash, splosh!
I defeat a huge rock
Now I push a gigantic ship out of my way
Splash! The ship flooded from my great power
I'm as strong as an ox
As I pass, I shoot huge waterfalls at the humans
As it gets dark, I calm down
Moving gently, gently, gently.

Mizan Uddin (10)
St Paul with St Luke Primary School, Bow

Calm Sea

The bubbly, calm, splashing sea
The relaxing, drumming sea
Although it loves swaying
Like running water
It feels as if I'm in
The dark, blue, deep sea.

First swaying calmly,
Now it's rushing, crashing
On the huge rocks!
As time went by
The sea was like a fly
A speedy car.

Suraiya Khatun (10)
St Paul with St Luke Primary School, Bow

The Calm River

The river swaying from side to side
A silky cover for the river to relax
The river is so peaceful for you to just chill out
Swish, bubble, bubble, the river in a calm, gentle voice
A stream moving along, gleaming in the sunlight
The sun shining bright to the river, *glitter, swish, whoosh*
The water shimmering in the thunderstorm
Frogs leaping on the edge of the river, jumping up and down
Boys and girls swimming in the water, *splish, splash* go the children
The river sways and goes to sleep calmly through the daylight . . .

Shaira Wahid (10)
St Paul with St Luke Primary School, Bow

Titanic

As I'm running with the breeze,
I fly up high over the Seven Seas,
When the boat called Titanic,
Floats on me, they start to panic,
Slowly sinking beneath,
Submerging like a falling leaf,
As they die,
People cry,
In the day,
People play,
Also surf,
On the day of their birth,
As I crash them with one of my waves,
They panic, but pretend to be brave,
I am as free as a bird, to do as I may,
I am soft, gentle, furious, as I sway!

Joel Davids (10)
St Paul with St Luke Primary School, Bow

Calm, Grumpy River

The sea is as calm as a lovely swimming pool
Shining like glitter everywhere
Flowing about, moving side to side
Swish, swoosh, splash!
Listen, as it chuckles nicely and calmly
Its sound is so quiet sometimes
You can't even hear it one bit
Sometimes it gets rough
It gets a bit grumpy
But it is calm.

Parnel Bemeh (10)
St Paul with St Luke Primary School, Bow

What Makes Me Happy

I'm happy
When my pet plays with me

I'm happy
When I go out

I'm happy
When I score a goal

I'm happy
When my friends play with me

I'm happy
When I go for a swim

I'm happy
When I play with my computer

I'm happy
When my teacher says, 'End of school.'

I'm happy
When just making other people happy.

Ajay Gill (9)
St Winifred's School, Southampton

Puppies

Oh, how I want a puppy!
Oh, what fun it would be
For my brother and me

Running and jumping
Playing and fighting
It would be so inviting

How to choose
I really don't know
One with brown fur
One with white
One with spots
One with fluffy ears
One with spiky ears

Oh, what fun it would be
To have my very own puppy.

Hershila Parmar (9)
St Winifred's School, Southampton

A Dream

I have a dream where the sun is out
Colourful bright rainbows in the light blue sky
It's summer again

Let's play in the park
Swings and see-saws, slides and ropes
What should we play with?

Lots to do, but so little time
It's almost time to go
The bright blue is turning dark
But let's do some more tomorrow.

But I'm awake
And it's not summer
It's cold, dark winter.

Emily Black (9)
St Winifred's School, Southampton

Tennis

Tennis is a fun sport
You can play it on a court
Federer is first
Nadal is second
Tennis is fun for one and all

Forehand, backhand, volley, serve
On a tennis court
You will observe

Fifteen-love
Now it's fifteen-all
Who knows the final score?
Thirty-fifteen
Thirty-all
Back and forth goes the ball
Forty-thirty
Game, set, all.

Simon Solecki (7)
St Winifred's School, Southampton

Tiger

Teeth as sharp as a sword
Tail as swift as a snake
Feet move at a hundred miles per hour

Eyes are as big as marbles
Staring through the grass
Teeth as are sharp as a knife

Razor-like claws lash at its prey
Strong, devious tail
Tripping up the unsuspecting victim

Last and go
No thought for the victim
The tiger.

Stephen Whorwood (10)
St Winifred's School, Southampton

Ice Skating

Chilly air, solid ice,
Swans calmly gliding,
Birds happily flying,
Dancers delicately prancing,
Here on frozen waters,
The ice skaters are skating.

Figures gliding, whizzing, zooming,
Round the frozen arena,
Dodging and darting,
Through the cold air,
Deflating balloons, erratic,
Shooting through the air.

As darkness falls, the festive lights flash on,
Shimmering shadows skating,
Around the cold, wintry rink.

Georgia Parker (10)
St Winifred's School, Southampton

Rage

Rage is like a bomb, ready to explode
Rage causes mass destruction
Rage starts fights!

Rage is a weapon
Rage is like a flame getting bigger
Rage starts wars!

Rage is the devil of emotions
Rage is powerful
Rage causes death!

Ben Marsh (11)
St Winifred's School, Southampton

The World

The sun: what is it?
It is a blushing eye,
Gazing over all of us.

The moon: what is it?
It is a face,
Smiling down on Earth from space.

Stars: what are they?
Stars are the children of the night,
Dots of hope, always with us.

Day: what is it?
Could it be a time, when we
Can all be seen for who we are?

Time: what is it?
Time is a thing no man can control,
A thing that goes so quickly and yet so slow.

Jessica Low (11)
St Winifred's School, Southampton

The Weather

The cold weather makes me sad
The wet weather makes me mad
The snowy weather makes me happy
The stormy weather makes me scared
The sunny weather makes me joyful
The icy weather makes me shivery
The windy weather makes me feel breathless

But I just love all kind of weather.

Samuel Riley (8)
St Winifred's School, Southampton

My First Pet

My first pet, what shall it be?
My first pet, should it be a bumblebee?

My first pet, a goldfish or two?
My first pet, I don't have a clue

My first pet, a cat or a dog?
My first pet, what about a frog?

My first pet, a type of bird?
What? A canary? Yes! that's good

My first pet, I hope
Will not have sharp claws

My first pet, I hope
Is as good as yours

My first pet, I just can't wait for
My first pet, will bring me happiness galore.

Louise King (9)
St Winifred's School, Southampton

Hamsters

Some hamsters are happy
Some hamsters are rude
Some hamsters are cool
And some hamsters are dudes

They hop and jump and throw themselves thus,
They nibble and nibble, fit to bust.
They ride on their wheel and never stop
Sometimes I think they might pop!

They eat bits of this and bits of that
Mine's even scared of the cat!
I think I saw one eating scrap
I like to imagine they have purses
So thank you for sharing my verses.

Francesca Mylod-Ford (8)
St Winifred's School, Southampton

My Brother

My brother is fourteen years of age
And has a terrible rage

He hogs the game
That I want to play

Then I try to get him off
But he just ignores me or hits me

Then I tell my mum
And I get the blame

But when his friends are round
He is suddenly nice

When his friends are nice to me
He makes fun of me

I probably don't need to say anymore
I think you understand, what he is like.

Frank Eardley (10)
St Winifred's School, Southampton

Killer Lioness

Fast and stealthy,
Queen of the jungle,
Menacing predator,
Stalks and kills her prey.
Escaping victims are pursued,
Her eyes are black and scrutinizing,
She uses her nose to track her dinner,
Her claws, so sharp, they cut like razor-sharp blades,
Even a tiger would be offended.

But when with her cubs,
She becomes a gentle mother.

Tristan Harley (10)
St Winifred's School, Southampton

My Sister

You might think sisters are annoying, greedy, selfish?

But not my sister
She's always willing to lend,
Recorders, poems, sweets and money.

She never pushes me or ignores me . . .

Sisters, boring? Not mine!

Her creative mind means spare time is fun!
We paint, we sew and we play games.

She makes us laugh,
Her joke telling is sublime.

She entertains us when she decides
To be a drama queen, stropping from room to room,
Huffing and puffing,
It is a sight to behold!

That's why I sort of like *my* sister.

Rachel Ellison (10)
St Winifred's School, Southampton

Taxi Joe

Man's best friend is also my best friend!
Meet Taxi Joe, the delightful dog!
With his long snout and his splodgy nose,
It's hard not to just fall in love with him.
The little bell on his collar, is so different to his size,
His long, floppy ears are so flexible,
So funny when he woofs in his sleep,
Taxi Joe is my colossal canine!

Euan Anderson (11)
St Winifred's School, Southampton

Birds

I see a swan, gliding down the stream,
Its feathers shine with a perfect gleam.
This elegant bird, with wings so white,
Dances down the river, in the golden sun.

I see a swallow, darting through the sky,
With wings as black as midnight.
A body, shaped with glorious curves,
Searching the land for food.

I see a gull, fishing in the sea,
A great sight to behold.
The sound resonates through the air,
An accompaniment to the soft *whoosh* of the waves.

Birds are everywhere, everywhere you go,
The kingfisher, the pigeon, all to see.

Birds are great, wouldn't you agree?

Reece Bridger (11)
St Winifred's School, Southampton

Tyrannosaurus Rex

Sharp teeth, angry eyes,
Grey armour, rough and coarse,
Big and tough, a meat eater.
Tail, long and hard,
His thunderous roar echoes around the miles,
His dead meat smell, drifts around the air,
He was the ruler of the dinosaurs.

Arman Miah (10)
St Winifred's School, Southampton

Full Time

Goalkeepers
    Defenders
        Midfielders
            And strikers
Come out of the tunnel,
Toss a coin to see who starts,
Kick-off in the middle.

Forty-five minutes in the first-half
Lots of fouls,
    Free kicks
        And penalties
Maybe even goals.

Fifteen minutes in, half-time

Second half,
More goals
    And different score lines
At the end of the match

Match over
Crowd goes home
    Full-time!

Arman Shabgard (9)
St Winifred's School, Southampton

Panther

Claws . . .
Razor-sharp,
As strong as ivory tusks,
As it rips through the jungle grass.

Teeth . . .
Fierce,
As red as blood,
As it sinks its teeth into its helpless victim.

Fur . . .
Dark, soft,
As black as the night sky.

Eyes . . .
Wide, evil, vicious,
As they twinkle in the dark.

The panther gets his kill,
He stands over his lifeless prey
Victorious.

Jack Handy (10)
St Winifred's School, Southampton

Raptor

I am Raptor, king of speed,
In a prehistoric forest.

Dark trees lurk around me,
Snakes, hissing as I go by.

With shiny teeth and a sensitive nose,
I look for prey, smelling for flesh.

Beware! For the T-rex, so sly,
Could be anywhere.

Waiting for me,
Darting through the forest.

A slow moving figure catches my eye,
A baby stegosaurus.

This should be an easy kill,
With one giant leap
And a quick flip of a sharp claw
I have my supper.

Adam Johnston (10)
St Winifred's School, Southampton

The Sun

The sun, the sun,
    Hot,
        Hot sun
Colours
   Red and orange
The heat
   Beating down on you
Oh, so hot
   Oh, so hot, I tell you
Dazzling,
   Blinding
With all different colours
The sun
   Lights up the sky
The morning sun's beams
Sprouting,
   Jumping,
      Leaping,
         Everywhere.

Georgia Moores (10)
St Winifred's School, Southampton

The Sweet Shop

Skipping on my way to school
I pass a shop that's really cool
I press my nose against the glass
And what I see makes me gasp!
There are rows and rows of big glass jars
Filled with sweets and goodie bars!

There are chubby gobstoppers and rhubarb rock,
Winter mixture which is very hot!
Cough candy twists and fizzy whizzy,
Scanning the shelves, my eyes are busy.

Can I spot the sherbet pips
Or should I try the lucky dips?
Rosy apples and chocolate limes,
'Come on,' said Mum, 'you're taking your time.'

So hard to choose, maybe aniseed balls?
If I could, I would have them all,
Jersey toffee and clotted cream fudge,
My sister, Jordy, gave me a nudge.

Look over here, I've found your favourite,
Flying saucers in ice cream colours,
Melt in the mouth, then a sherbet fizz,
I really think they are the biz!

I queue at the counter and pay for my sweets,
Mrs Macreedy gives me a treat,
Try this sherbet lemon,
I thought it tasted just like Heaven,
I say goodbye and leave by the door,
It won't be long before I'm back for more!

Ellie Turl (10)
St Winifred's School, Southampton

Maths

Maths, maths, x2, x3, x4
                      And more
Maths, maths, +2, +3, +4
                      And more
Maths, maths, ÷2, ÷3, ÷4
                      And more
Maths, maths, -2, -3, -4
                      And more
Maths, maths, it's money questions
                      And more
Maths, maths, it's weighing items
                      And more
Maths, maths, it's telling the time
                      And more
Maths, maths, to some people
It *can* be quite a chore
                But to me, maths is not a bore!

Martinez Hart (8)
St Winifred's School, Southampton

The Wind

The wind blowing with all its might
The wind flowing gently in the air
Two bits of wind colliding
Wobbling the leaves on the trees
The wind crashing against the window
Flipping and dancing through the air
The wind zapping everything
The wind shivering in the air
The wind flying across the window
The wind swirling through the soft air.

Sam Verran (8)
Shiplake CE Primary School, Henley on Thames

The Wind

The wind is zooming very fast,
Dashing quick as it can.
Pushing normal people away,
Then blowing the green grass.

The wind is tickling everyone on the neck,
Whooshing the flowers together.
The wind is swooshing oak trees away,
The wind is rushing so quickly at speed.
Then clashing things down,
The wind is crashing an old house.
Swooping branching around,
The wind is as freezing cold as ice.

Paul Lyon (8)
Shiplake CE Primary School, Henley on Thames

The Wind

The wind is zooming in the sky
The branches are moving too
There's wind shooting against the bark
The creeping grass is swaying as well
The branches are flaming too
The moon is whistling as well
The wind is shooting in the air
The wind is prancing and dancing around the tree
There's hail crashing into nests
The wind is zooming around the birds
The wind is crashing down the trees
The wind is lashing the ponds
There's also shimmering rain.

Isabella Bull (7)
Shiplake CE Primary School, Henley on Thames

The Wind

The bouncing, pouncing, leaping wind,
Sending grass flying over fields,
Gently pushing swings back and forth,
Back and forth,
Freezing your cheeks and turning them pink,
Blowing soggy leaves everywhere,
Sneaking up behind you and . . . *boo!*
It pushes you over,
You land with a thud on the floor,
But the wind is also very calm
And is very gentle,
It blows very nicely in the fields
And blows all the dead leaves away in autumn,
So never blame the wind for wounding you,
For it will help you.

Ella Wandless (8)
Shiplake CE Primary School, Henley on Thames

The Wind

The wind booms against the twigs
The wind zooms
The wind shoots across
Pushes the soggy trees
The wind squeezes people
Sounds loud *and louder*
The wind blows people over
The wind bashes cupboards open and shut
The wind break mugs
The wind is noise
The wind freezes people
The wind sways.

Rosanna Pentecost (8)
Shiplake CE Primary School, Henley on Thames

The Wind

Strong, huffing and puffing wind
As if wanting to blow down an old house
Big, dashing leaves like on sports day
Fast, zooming wind like a racing car
Cold, twisting wind like a corkscrew
Fast, whooshing wind like a racing car
Nice dancing and prancing like they were at a disco
Gently swirling leaves like a merry-go-round
Funny wiggling tree branches like worms
Cold, blowing wind like breathing
Strong, pushing wind like it was playing with the trees
Scary, whistling wind like someone whistling
Very breezy coldness, like Antarctica.

Hattie Foster (7)
Shiplake CE Primary School, Henley on Thames

Wind

The wind rustling the trees of the oak tree
The wind flutters the leaves
The wind buffeting in and out
The wind squeezing people
The wind smashes windows
The wind prances and dances the waves
The wind sways the trees
The wind creaks the wood
The wind zooms around with the grey air.

Leah Parry-Williamson (7)
Shiplake CE Primary School, Henley on Thames

The Wind

The wind creeping behind people so they get scared
The banging trees like a fun game
The jumping grass like a trampoline
The wind pushing trees so that they bang
The wind zooming air as a great game
The wind bashing old people walking to the shops
The wind pushing walls that are shiny and brown
The wind banging walls that are wobbly
The wind slashing people so that they fall
The wind pushing houses so that they fall
The wind turning tables like a big knot
The wind hitting trees like a wrestling match
The wind rushing in rooms because it's cold
The wind shooting air like a race track
The wind dancing and prancing across the road like a ballet floor.

Lorna Cousins (8)
Shiplake CE Primary School, Henley on Thames

The Wind

I can see the wind pulling trees towards me
I can hear the wind banging against the trees
I can see the wind shaking the house
I can hear oak trees banging together
I can see the wind swaying and clanging
I can see the wind pushing the clouds away
I can hear the wind breathing.

Chloe Shorter (7)
Shiplake CE Primary School, Henley on Thames

The Wind

Wind smashing windows
Trying to break them.
Wind bashing trees
Trying to break the tree.

The cold wind
Making animals shiver.
Wind climbing chairs
Walking up a mountain.

The wind flying
Like you're on top of a mountain.

Wind listening to the clouds
To know if rain was going to come.

Quin Wagner-Piggott (7)
Shiplake CE Primary School, Henley on Thames

The Wind

The wind fights against houses
The wind breaks thick branches off trees
  The wind dashes past windows
The wind bashes walls
The wind zooms past fences
The wind cracks buildings
The wind crunches trees
The wind pushes houses
The wind shakes houses
The wind bangs trees.

Harry Waiton (8)
Shiplake CE Primary School, Henley on Thames

Jungle Sounds

In the emerald bay of Bengal
The silent tiger advances through the jungle

He can hear ants plodding carefully in the direction of the canopy
And baboons as vibrant as macaws, hooting from a huge tree

He can catch frogs hopping
And crickets bouncing

With snakes zigzagging through the undergrowth
Over the top, he can hear elephants trumpeting

Rhinos charging with hippos wallowing
Human guns piercing the atmosphere

Then the jungle noise starts all over again
And the last creature to be heard, is the peacock trilling

After the last couple of gunshots, the jungle noise is silent
Apart from the odd, cracking twig.

David Griffiths (9)
West Chiltington Primary School, Pulborough

Sounds Of The Forest

Deep in the early morning undergrowth
Tiger silently awakes with loud sounds far away
The forest is stirring.

I hear the monkey's tail
Curling around the mowa tree.

I hear the slithering of the snake
Going up the narrow tree.

I hear the calling of the toucan
Up high in the trees.

The crunch of the leaves
Falling from the nearby trees.

I hear the ripple of the lake
As the elephant washes himself in it.

All went quiet, as tiger laid down
He needed a bit of a snooze, so he dozed off.

Bethany Willmer (10)
West Chiltington Primary School, Pulborough

The Sound Of The Forest

Prowling as silently as the lime-green grass blowing in the wind
A stripy tiger can hear many unusual sounds in the great forest.

The sound of pebbles being washed up on the bank
Can even block out the splashing of the rapid river.

Speedily, the great, green grasshopper
Grinds its gangly legs to make a scratchy tune.

A gurgling gulp from a gecko
Hiding in the emerald forest.

A spider scuttling towards its sticky web
To check for unlucky prey.

The snapping of a chestnut-brown stick
Being trodden on by a growling tiger.

Suddenly, the sounds start to die away and then - all was silence
The tiger turned and peered into the eerie darkness . . .

Thomas Ranger (9)
West Chiltington Primary School, Pulborough

Living Animals

The significant turtle hovered
Across the deep ocean

Uncertain tiger did not know
What to do

Running rabbit sprinted
Under the tall, swinging grass

The overweight crocodile gleamed
At the female crocodile

Lonely antelope searching in vain
For the rest of his herd

Elegant elephants stamping
Across the desert ground.

Brandon La Roche (10)
West Chiltington Primary School, Pulborough

I'm Hearing

Deep in the coal-black tangled forest,
The tigress listened carefully, prowling through the forest.

I'm hearing caterpillar's body crackling,
As it proceeds through the dusty damp forest.

I'm hearing birds silently resting on a branch
Looking down at tiny fragile worms.

I'm hearing the flower petals opening
In a silent whisper.

I'm hearing the lonely footsteps of a hedgehog
Wandering around all the trees.

I'm hearing a deserted cocoon hanging by a thin thread
Falling every second, opening just slightly more.

I'm hearing the grass snake slithering up and down
And through the green grass and leaves.

I'm hearing a fish gliding through the misty water
Munching on the lake's small dead weeds.

As night falls, the tangled forest sleeps silently
Like a breath of wind.

Eliza Russell (10)
West Chiltington Primary School, Pulborough

Elephant

Elephant trumpeting, slurping
Monkey sprinting, yelling, chewing
Macaw alarming, calling, munching
Frog croaking, hopping, scoffing
Antelope chomping, swallowing
Jackal scavenging and sniffing
King cobra hissing and spitting
Fox fighting chicken-chasing
Horse galloping and cantering
Camel spitting and chewing.

Josh Hutchison (10)
West Chiltington Primary School, Pulborough

The Jungle

Deep in the amber-green forest,
A tiger prowls alone and hears unusual noises.

The enormous screech of a monkey,
In tortuous pain.

The cackle of curious kookaburra
In the main.

The moan of a young monkey
Miraculously involved in a fight with his parents.

There were parrots squawking
Scarcely in the sky.

Soon, all the noises had faded away into muted silence
And the tiger scarpered home.

Emily Cooperwaite (10)
West Chiltington Primary School, Pulborough

Sounds Of The Forest

Tiger begins his silent journey
Through the deep, early morning undergrowth.

I can hear the rustling of the branches
From the nearby trees.

The ripple from the crystal-clear lake
I can hear the flowers creeping from up above the grass.

The murmur from an insect down below
Suddenly, the forest quietened as the tiger padded back to his den
To devour his food.

Rhianna-Marie Ovenden (9)
West Chiltington Primary School, Pulborough

Sounds In The Forest

Prowling tiger
Slowly pads through the tangly forest
Silently looking for prey.

Tiger hears ants padding carefully
And speeding towards the canopy.

Tiger listens to flighty fish diving
In and out of the transparent pool.

Tiger eavesdrops on the birds high in the trees
Singing like an orchestra.

Tiger learns the language of calling elephants
Trumpeting in the far distance.

There are so many sounds, but Tiger still has found no prey
And Tiger wearily drags himself home.

Isabel Fitzgibbon (9)
West Chiltington Primary School, Pulborough

Sounds In The Forest

Deep in the early morning shimmers
Tiger starts his perilous prowl in the lush undergrowth.

Then he hears the sudden sound of a violent Venus flytrap
Silently suffocating its prey.

The crackling of the rhino's heavy feet crushing the layer of leaves
Dry from the burning sun.

The background sound of the magnificent elephant
Ripping the vibrant green branches off the tree
That was as big as the Eiffel Tower.

Tiger goes back to his home and rests
Whilst thinking about the next noisy day.

William Jeffries (9)
West Chiltington Primary School, Pulborough

Jungle Walk

A jungle walk through the green undergrowth
Where animals thrive and plants flourish

I can hear the mighty lion roar
Like a fighter jet engine

I can hear a giraffe's tongue
Wrap around a branch like a lasso

I can hear a snake slithering through the leaves
As quietly as an assassin

I can hear a herd of elephants
Trumpeting like an orchestra

I can hear the crunching
Of the lizard's skin shedding

I can hear an antelope's skin
Being pierced by a rhino's horn

In the jungle, it's fascinating the sounds you hear
The sights you see
It's amazing in the jungle
As amazing as can be.

George Richardson (10)
West Chiltington Primary School, Pulborough

In The Jungle

Early in the morning
The sun was like silk,
The lime-green forest was alive.

Peacocks shining, emerald eyes,
Glowing in the sun's rays.

Rhino's outstanding armour,
Bouncing off the sun's beams.

Monkeys umbrella tails,
Gliding and swinging from tree to tree.

Elephant charging,
Into calm water.

Army ant columns marching,
One by one.

Parrot's deafening screams,
Blasting sound waves through the air.

Night falls, there's no sun,
Only the light from the moon.

Matthew Solomon (10)
West Chiltington Primary School, Pulborough

Animal Noises

The stripy tiger heard the cricket
Buzzing and bouncing across the grass

The bellowing noise, screeching cricket
Bounced around the tiger's paws

Going over the top
The cricket stared and wound the tiger up

The birds shrieked, the elephant bellowed
The cricket ran away

He ran and ran through the bushes
Past his house, across the river

He snuggled in close and fell asleep
In the safety of his mum.

Josh Steggles (9)
West Chiltington Primary School, Pulborough

The Beginning Of The Amazing Planet Earth

The spread of a ripple
Shimmering in the bright water

The sound of a petal
Screaming in the bright moon, yelling for help.

A waving whisker from an angry cat
Ready to chase a minute mouse.

A tiger waiting to pounce
On its hot prey covered in sweat.

The crackling lava waiting to explode
And run down like streams of hot and smooth treacle.

Tim Craig (9)
West Chiltington Primary School, Pulborough

Young Writers Information

We hope you have enjoyed reading this book - and that you will continue to enjoy it in the coming years.

If you like reading and writing poetry drop us a line, or give us a call, and we'll send you a free information pack.

Alternatively if you would like to order further copies of this book or any of our other titles, then please give us a call or log onto our website at www.youngwriters.co.uk

**Young Writers Information
Remus House
Coltsfoot Drive
Peterborough
PE2 9JX**

(01733) 890066